The
Youth Baseball
Bible

What people are saying about Dan Gray and his book:

"Although I have played, coached and managed in the Major Leagues, one of the hardest things I have ever done is relinquish baseball coaching responsibilities for my own son. Then along came Dan Gray. As a youth, college and pro player, Dan honed his natural feel for the game. He knows and loves baseball. More importantly, Dan has an indescribable, immeasurable and unrivaled ability to communicate with and develop kids. This book expertly guides the reader through the basics of coaching youth baseball. Its impact goes far beyond the game's clinical and technical requirements: it teaches adults how to be human toward children. Dan encourages the concept of effective and meaningful communication, including appropriate timing, tone and purpose. I could not have found a better coach for my own son, and anyone seeking advice would benefit from reading and relying on Dan's carefully crafted book."

—Joe Girardi, three-time World Series Champion as player (Yankees), 2006 N.L. Manager of the Year (Marlins), Yankees Manager (2008–2017) and 2009 World Series Champions

"Dan's work ethic and commitment to his craft have always shined through and continue to drive his success. Having known Dan for 20 years, it's hard to think of other people who match his ability to connect with young athletes. Throughout his success and growth, the thing that has remained most apparent to me is the type of person that Dan is, and his relationship with my family and me mean the world to us."

—Jeremy Zoll, Director, Minor League Operations Minnesota Twins

"I met Dan almost 12 years ago when I was looking for baseball instruction for my son. Not only has Dan made an impact on both my boys, he has become a friend. He is just a great guy and knows his baseball. I have had the opportunity to bring clients to see Dan and a co-worker who pitched in the big leagues for 17 years as well whose comment on Dan was, "Great guy and seems like a good baseball guy, and not a nut like so many." Enough said."

—Bobby Barad, Dad and pro baseball agent, Excel Sports Management

"As an active player with the Yankees, I spent many an off-season at Dan's ProSwing facility in Mt. Kisco working on my swing, and staying sharp and in shape through those cold Westchester, NY winters. As I meticulously did my work in his cages, I could see Dan was doing his work too – impacting thousands of young players, along with parents and coaches, with his incredible knowledge and wisdom from playing the game at a high level from Little league through AAA, and now for years as one of its top instructors.

Baseball is arguably one of the most difficult sports to play and excel at, which in turn makes it one of the most difficult to teach. In this book, Dan brilliantly breaks down all the aspects of teaching this great game to your kids, and as a coach, how to build a team of well-rounded and fundamentally sound players – and makes sure it includes the most important part - having fun doing so!

Follow closely Dan's instruction and techniques in the book, be patient and persistent with your kids, and the results will follow. Then, you can take pride in succeeding at what Dan has accomplished in his life in baseball – developing the best players, teammates, and young men and women of character and sportsmanship."

—Bernie Williams, five-time All-Star, AL Batting Champion, four-time Gold Glove winner and four-time World Series Champion

"The first time I walked into ProSwing, I could tell it's a family environment. The people and the atmosphere are so caring and genuine it's hard to find that nowadays. The first time I met Dan, within two minutes we were making jokes and I felt like I could tell him my life story. He listens with so much patience and genuinely takes the time to breakdown every word with a response full of wisdom and encouragement. He has been not only a mentor and baseball coach but a life coach. His knowledge comes from his love of the game and all the lessons learned from it. Not to mention the amount of time he's put into his research on the biomechanics of a swing, the ways to break down and re-build the swing accordingly, how to express those instructions with different tactics based on the person he is dealing with and what he analyzes is the best way for that person to retain and execute that information. He is the best hitting coach I have worked with next to Kevin Long, and I have grown up around the game my entire life. I listen to every word out of Dan's mouth because I know that it is meaningful, has a purpose, and will make me a better hitter and person."

—Lee Mazilli Jr.

"The baseball community, on both the professional and amateur level, as large as it seems, it is actually quite small. Experience, reputation and character matter—people know the real deal baseball guys. Dan Gray is one of those guys, the best and the brightest. Having coached him during my years with the L.A. Dodgers I knew, even at his young age, he was something special, as a player and more importantly as a person. Years later he worked side by side with me as an instructor in my baseball school in northern New Jersey. He is as passionate and knowledgeable in regard to America's pastime as anyone I've met over my many years playing and coaching. His hands on approach, love for the game and unique perspective make him the ideal leader for instruction and advice to players and coaches of all backgrounds and interests."

—Garett Teel, former MLB player and owner, Teels Baseball & Softball Training Center

"Dan's simple hitting approach and methods have allowed me to make the necessary adjustments to help "re-discover" my swing and hopefully, get myself back to the major leagues very soon."

—Mike Olt, Texas Rangers 2012, Chicago Cubs 2014-2015, Chicago White Sox 2015

The
Youth Baseball
Bible

The definitive guide to coaching,
mastering and enjoying youth baseball

Dan Gray
Former LA Dodgers Pro

THE YOUTH BASEBALL BIBLE: THE DEFINITIVE GUIDE TO COACHING, MASTERING AND ENJOYING YOUTH BASEBALL

ISBN: 978-0-578-41309-9

Book design by Sarah E. Holroyd (https://sleepingcatbooks.com)
Cover design by Lucas Tyson and Sarah E. Holroyd

Acknowledgments

Most successful people in life will tell you that their achievements are not a solo effort. I believe that baseball is a microcosm for life in general, nurturing and developing the qualities necessary to perpetuate passion and drive for ALL endeavors waiting to be explored and conquered. My journey has been no different...many people have shaped my baseball life and the good fortune of being able to stay involved in the greatest game in the world over the past 40 years. I would like to take the time to thank some of those who have inspired me to help inspire others:

Mom & Dad—My heros...My mentors...My biggest fans...My everything. You and me against the world!

Nana & Poppa—My life lessons, outlook on life and how to treat people came from you. I miss you guys every day.

Aunt Joan & Uncle Steve—your independent thinking, constant encouragement and support, and ability to always make me laugh will forever hold a special place in my heart.

My wife & sons DJ and Adam—Thank you for your constant support and allowing me to pursue my passion. Your patience and sacrifice is humbling and I love you guys more than you know.

Charlie Conway—My co-coach on and off the field. You are the brother I never had and I am still trying to work on being half the man you are. Your input and wisdom during this process has been invaluable.

Asher Lee-Tyson and Ethan Lee-Tyson—Your writing assistance and editing have been invaluable. You have made me more insightful and I can't thank you enough for your hard work and dedication in making this book a reality. And special thanks to Judy Lee for her excellent work taking the photos.

Garrett Teel—My dear friend and mentor within the baseball instructional industry. Thanks for showing me, on a daily basis, how to stay true to the purpose and ALWAYS make the kids the number one priority.

Joe Girardi—Thank you for trusting me with your son, Dante. Your class, professionalism, generosity and grace greatly outweigh your vast baseball knowledge. You're one of the good guys who treats people the right way.

L.A. Dodgers Organization & Coaches—I am forever grateful to have been drafted by the best teaching organization in the game. Thank you for showing me what it took to be a professional player, but more importantly, building the foundation of knowledge for me that I have been fortunate enough to pass along to my players for the past 28 years.

ProSwing Instructors—MY EXTENDED FAMILY! We have shared the grind together for many years through the ups and downs. The bond we share, philosophies we teach, and deep friendships we continue to develop are dear to my heart. TO THE GREATEST BASEBALL STAFF—I applaud and salute you.

ProSwing Players & Their Families—THANK YOU! For allowing me the opportunity to be a part of your lives. The most rewarding part of my job is to watch my kids take the game as far as they can and then take from their learned experiences with us, the tools to become outstanding people. I am acutely aware of the honor and privilege it is to be entrusted with your kids! And I will never take that responsibility lightly. Special thanks to Adam Agresti, James Weber and Jack DeAngelis for their help with the many photos throughout this book.

About Dan Gray

Dan's love of baseball started way back when he was a Little Leaguer in the Bronx, NY. His passion for the game continued through his high school years at The Bronx High School of Science where he was selected to the All-City team his senior year. It was during his collegiate experience at Binghamton University where he became the first player in school history to be chosen for the amateur draft, when the Los Angeles Dodgers selected him in the 7th round.

By most accounts, the Los Angeles Dodgers were considered the premier teaching and player development organization in all of baseball at the time. "The Dodger Way" of playing the game became the foundation and focal point for Dan's instructional template following the end of his playing career.

Currently, Dan is the owner of the ProSwing Baseball & Softball Training Center in Mount Kisco, NY which opened in 2002. The second ProSwing facility, opened in 2009, is located in Port Chester, NY.

"The daily mission is to create a comfortable learning environment that enhances knowledge and passion for the game and accelerates personal satisfaction and growth. Every day I use baseball as the vehicle to improve each player's self-esteem in helping become the best player and person possible," says Dan.

To date, Dan has been quoted in many outlets such as *The New York Times*, *The Westchester Business Journal* and *The Journal News*. In addition, he has been a featured guest speaker on CNN, WFAN, ESPN radio, WXRK and New York 1. These outlets, along with his involvement in over 200 coaches clinics, have highlighted several of Dan's favorite topics, such as player development, youth sports and parental involvement, youth baseball issues, steroids in baseball—youth perspective, off season baseball training routines, and many others.

A Note from Dan

For those of us fortunate enough to have played or coached the great game of baseball, the feeling of hitting the game-winning home run or leading a group of players to an important win or championship is indescribable. However, at the youth level, ballplayers and coaches should focus and emphasize the PROCESS over the RESULT.

This process begins with the commitment to becoming the best you can be, while keeping a positive attitude and high level of enjoyment. Second, an action plan should be put in place in order to effectively realize your commitment. At this point, you are ready to follow the action plan by PRACTICE, with the understanding that you will have to alter or modify your course based on any obstacles or bumps in the road that impede progress. Finally, through assessment and correction, you can begin to PERFECT your overall process to maximize performance.

Once you have done this, YOUR BEST BASEBALL IS AHEAD OF YOU. Whether you are a player or coach, YOUR process will begin to INSPIRE others to follow suit. Then, the TEAM will be on its way to playing to its full potential.

TRAIN . . . EDUCATE . . . INSPIRE!!!

—Dan Gray

CONTENTS

Chapter 1

Introduction

If you're reading this, then you are probably about to embark on a youth baseball coaching experience, and chances are, you have no idea what to expect! Perhaps a family member or friend talked you into this, and being the person you are, you agreed. Or, you may simply have kids of your own with whom you wish to share the wonderful game of baseball. (I also hope that some young players themselves will take an interest in reading this book.)

You probably know a little something about the game, but you just aren't sure where to begin. In the pages that follow, you will receive a crash course in understanding baseball beginning at the most basic levels and rapidly progressing from there.

I'm a baseball guy. I've been around baseball ever since I can remember. As a kid growing up in the Bronx, NY, baseball was all I looked forward to every day after school, on the weekends, and all summer long. Playing ball in high school and college helped prepare me for a professional baseball career. As a pro (I was drafted by the Los Angeles Dodgers in the 7th round), not only was I able to grow as a player from simply playing baseball, I was fortunate enough to be around some of the best baseball minds in the game. Over the years that followed my playing days, I've had many enlightening conversations with some of the premiere players and coaches of our generation. I've studied this great game with pinpoint attention to details, and I've used my accumulated knowledge to teach and coach thousands of players of every age for more than two decades.

This book is a natural next step in my own career—a way to share some of my knowledge and experiences with you so that your sons and players will one day look back and remember how you helped them grow as a baseball player and as a person.

Baseball is a gift. Luckily, it is a gift that we can all enjoy and share together. Best wishes as you begin your journey as a baseball parent and coach!

Chapter 2

I'm the coach...now what?

Congratulations, coach! Ask anyone who's ever coached a group of kids before, and they will tell you that it's anything but easy, but the rewards can be priceless. There are a great number of things to get done before the first pitch, so let's get started!

Whether you're going to be coaching a team, or simply sharing baseball with your own kids and helping them to appreciate and get the most out of the game, the advice in this chapter will help you.

Philosophy & Goal Setting

One of the first things a coach needs to do is to set realistic goals within the constraints of their organization and league. There are countless variables that exist as a coach, such as roster size, age, player ability, budget, practice time, equipment and field resources, etc. Once you've identified the scope of your resources, you can then begin to plan out your season. A good place to begin is to develop a baseball coaching philosophy that will guide you throughout the season.

Regardless of the goals that are set, the overarching philosophy should be to create a positive, safe learning environment in order for all of the players to get the most out of the experience. A coach derives satisfaction not only from watching their best player perform in a clutch situation, but also from nurturing players with less talent to achieve things even they didn't think were possible at the beginning of the season. Each and every player should feel valued, and that they play an important role on the team.

Most coaches will agree that the overall baseball goal is to maximize every player's performance in order to achieve team success. In order to do this, the players all need to "buy in" to the coach's philosophy. Therefore, the coach's message should include the 3 C's: clear, concise, and consistent. Remember, as a coach you're not only teaching baseball skills, but you're also a major influence on your players in terms of character development and self-esteem.

Communication

One of the most important roles as a coach is to be an effective communicator. Several lines of communication must be open between you and:

- Your players

- Parents/Guardians

- Your staff (assistant coaches, etc.)

- Other coaches

- Umpires

- League/Tournament officials

The most important line of communication lies between the coach and the player. Each kid on your team must understand that you are the coach and the final decision maker, and that they need to respect your role as such. However, it is equally important for the coach to understand that each player has a voice of their own. For example, if a player isn't sure how to hold a runner on at first base because they've never played first before, he should be able to feel comfortable asking the coach to help out. It's really about the player feeling that you are approachable, and that you are receptive to the players' questions about the game and about their role.

As you plan your practices and pre-game routines, keep every player engaged. Be sure to communicate with each player as often as possible so that their role is clear, and their standing on the team is validated. Effectively communicating your plan will go a long way and will reduce the need to answer questions along the way. When a player asks you in the second inning, "Coach, when am I going in the game?" it seems like an annoying question, but it's natural for a kid to wonder if they don't know. They may not have the "filter" to understand that you have a lot of other things on your mind at that moment, and that their playing time is not at the top of the list! So, to avoid this, always let your players know what your plan for them that day is (to the extent that you are able). If you're not sure about if/when a player will be used (game situations often dictate these decisions), then let players know this before the game.

It is just as important to communicate effectively to your players during practices. This includes being specific about what you want your players to do from warm up until the very end of practice. Always model proper techniques for your players prior to drills until you know that players understand your expectations. Don't assume that players know how to take a proper lead, or where to go in a cutoff situation, or even how to properly throw a baseball. Remember, a coach is a teacher, and it is your role to help every player to become better.

During drills, let players know not just what they are doing incorrectly, but reinforce what they are doing correctly. And most importantly, keep your comments constructive and instructive rather than derogatory and destructive. Countless coaches have prematurely ended young players' careers by simply being unnecessarily critical of a player's ability or performance. The game is meant to be a positive and enjoyable learning experience for your kids, and if you are committed to this end, you will most likely communicate this to all of your players.

Finally, a word about how and when to say something, and when not to say something to your team or a player. Coaches often feel the need to give immediate feedback (often in the form of yelling across the field during a game). This isn't always an effective way to teach the game to kids. Some encouraging reminders keep things positive for your players, and often yields positive results. Negative criticism usually has the opposite effect. Sometimes it's best to pull your player aside after an inning or after the game to discuss what happened. (Some coaches keep a short list of problem areas they observe during a game and then discuss those topics with the team in its next practice.)

Here is one example of a game situation, and how a coach can handle it.

Situation: Your 11-year old team is down 2-1 late in the game. The bases are loaded with 2 outs, and your batter has a 3-1 count. The next pitch is up around eye level, and he swings & pops the ball up for the final out.

Coach One Response: The coach is clearly disgusted, throws his arms up in the air and loudly yells out toward the player, "What are you swinging at? That was ball 4!" The player jogs back to the dugout with his head down, grabs his glove, and goes back to onto the field with his shoulders shrugged.

Coach Two Response: The coach later calls the player over and calmly and privately asks, "What pitch were you looking for in that situation?" The player responds, "A good pitch that I can hit hard somewhere." The coach reinforces the right approach, and then says, "OK, but we have to be more selective up there and not try and do too much. Let's go out there and play solid defense and get 'em next time." The player understands, runs back onto the field and gets ready for the defensive half of the inning.

Clearly there are a variety of ways in which a coach can handle this sort of situation. Most likely the player will know his mistake. Adding further embarrassment by doing what Coach One did doesn't help. The player will feel worse about himself and is susceptible to making an error in the next inning because he's still thinking about the last at-bat. Coach Two's response is much more productive mainly because the coach uses the situation as a teaching opportunity. The player is obviously not trying to make an out, and the coach realizes that fact. Communicating with the player in this manner potentially turns a negative result into something positive for the player, and ultimately for the team. The player will probably be in that situation again sometime down the road, and you want him to be confident in his abilities the next time rather than worrying about failing again. As we will discuss later on, baseball is a game of failure – and dealing with that reality is a challenge all ball players must face. It is the coach's role and responsibility to help every player overcome their own failures to become a better ball player, which in turn makes the team better.

Finally, expect that some players will try your patience – guaranteed! Be careful how you handle situations that arise when a player isn't living up to your expectations. Remember that YOU are the adult and maintain a respectful tone. Don't ever engage in a back-and-forth verbal battle with a player, and do not ever embarrass a player. There is nothing to be gained from this. Parents, other players, and fans are watching and listening to you at all times, and you won't maintain the respect of everyone involved with your team if you embrace confrontation.

When it comes to parents and families, it is a must for a coach to effectively communicate with them from the get go. As soon as the team is set, parents will thirst for information. Questions are inevitable, and a coach can save time and energy by providing parents with the information they need. Although they won't throw a pitch, hit a ball, or field a grounder, parents do play an important role on your team, and therefore should be considered a part of the team.

Most coaches miss an important opportunity at the beginning of each season, most likely because there are lots of other things to worry about. However, a pre-season meeting with parents/guardians as a group can be immensely helpful to you. It will provide an opportunity for you to share all of the logistical information they need, and it can provide you with a forum to explain what their role is as a baseball parent on your team. How many stories have you heard about parents overstepping their boundaries? If the boundaries are not set, then it's difficult to establish your expectations later on.

Here's a list of topics of communication a coach should share with families:

- Practice and game schedule

- Player clothing & equipment expectations

- Expectations of players and families

- How to get in touch with you (phone/email/etc.)

- Your coaching philosophy

Once you have laid everything out for the season, you are on your way. As the season progresses, expect that you will need to keep an ongoing line of communication with families. Schedule changes, weather issues, travel plans, and individual player concerns are just a few of the topics you should prepare to discuss with parents.

Some topics are purely informational and are easy to handle. But when it comes to issues regarding individual players (such as playing time, positions, etc.), it's a much slipperier slope. It's crucial to keep in mind that parents are inherently biased, and it's normal to expect them to be partial to their own child. As long as you allow your parents an avenue to discuss their concerns, it will help alleviate potential problems.

Parents tend to approach these discussions in a variety of ways. Most are sincere and respectful, and others can be more direct and confrontational. Be upfront about how and when parents should approach you about their issues. Parents should know that any time during a game is NOT a good time to discuss playing time or what position they think their kid should play. The only time a parent should have any direct communication with a coach during a game is if there is a safety or injury concern. Other issues can wait until after the game.

As the coach, do all that you can to separate your own personal feelings about parents from your decisions as a coach. It may not be easy, but once it appears that you are giving preferential treatment toward a player whose parent is a friend/buddy/ally, it will inevitably cause dissention among the other parents and potentially the players. This is never good. You need to remain as impartial as you can, and make coaching decisions based on what YOU think is best for the players and for your team.

When talking with parents about their child and their role on the team, be open and honest with them. Allow parents to have their say and share with them your perspective as well. Remember to keep your decisions in line with your coaching philosophy. Sometimes parents can shed light on something and it will be helpful to you. Always assure parents that your coaching decisions are based on a combination of factors, all of which are your best attempt to help every player on your team succeed. By taking a positive, proactive approach to communicating with your parents, you will earn their respect as a coach, and it will go a long way toward making your season enjoyable for all.

Most coaches have a "staff"—whether it be another parent volunteer or two, or an assistant coach. One very important conversation you should have prior to the season is with your assistant(s). An honest conversation about how you would like to run the team is crucial to get the season off to a good start. If you are on the same page beginning with the first practice, the players, parents, and any other observers of your team will get a positive impression about where the team is headed. Discuss all aspects of the season at your initial meeting, such as:

- Coaching philosophy

- Practice/game schedule

- The role of each coach (during games & practices)

- Logistics (such as equipment & travel)

- Your team (players, positions, etc.).

Having a staff that thinks similarly about the game as you do will prove invaluable as the season goes along. There will be plenty of times where you will need to make an important decision, and it's always good to bounce ideas off someone you trust. Also, if you have a scheduling conflict where you will be late or if you need to miss a practice or game, your staff should be able to run things in the same basic way you would. Consistency is the goal, and your players and parents deserve a consistent coaching staff.

Beyond the core people of your team (players, parents, staff), you will also need to communicate effectively with folks outside your organization. Prepare to interact with lots of different people with lots of different personalities! Whether its opposing coaches, league officials, umpires, or even fans, always keep in mind that you are the main representative of your team. You are the leader, and people take cues from you, therefore it's important to keep in mind that you always want to represent yourself and your organization in a respectful and consistent manner.

When it comes to umpires, youth coaches must always keep in mind that umpiring is not likely to be the primary way they make these people make their living (some may even be older kids who are trying to make a few extra bucks). Throughout the history of the game, umpires at every level have incurred the wrath of players, coaches, and fans alike. It's a no-win job. So, when you disagree with the ump, be sure to pick and choose carefully when and how you approach them. Keep everything in perspective. You're not a major league manager (at least not yet), and your players are not in the pros.

The key thing to keep in mind is respect. You're allowed to disagree with the umpire, without question. But remember that if you go out and challenge the ump, everyone will be watching, and it's more important to earn the respect of the ump, your players, your parents, and the fans than it is to get your frustration off your chest. Let the ump know that you think they missed a call in a cool and calm manner and move on. Don't expect the ump to change a call – it hardly ever happens. Furthermore, your actions will speak volumes to your players. If you fly off the handle, rant and rave and kick dirt on the plate, your players will think that's acceptable. If you handle it properly, your players will know that you're standing up for them but doing it in a respectful manner.

Remember, as a coach, there's a bigger picture beyond baseball, and you're a key figure in developing your players as people. The way in which you communicate with others may be the most important thing you do as a coach. Many times in baseball as in other areas of life, it's not just about what you do, but how you do it.

Role Model

Whether you want to be considered a role model or not, as a coach you are automatically thrust into that position. The amount of time that you spend with your players during a season is commensurate to spending time with close family members. Thus, impressionable young ballplayers will regularly be watching and listening to what you do and say. It's unavoidable! Therefore, embrace the opportunity to make an impact on your players beyond the game of baseball.

From the first practice to the last pitch of the last game, your demeanor is the key factor in how you present yourself as a leader. Do you get into heated arguments with umpires, or do you understand that bad calls are part of the game? The way you comport yourself in the role as coach will directly affect both the attitude of each player, and direction your team takes.

⊘ ⊘ ⊘ ⊘ ⊘ ⊘ ⊘ **Story from Dan** ⊘ ⊘ ⊘ ⊘ ⊘ ⊘ ⊘

Joe Girardi's son Dante played for me a couple of years. Joe was outstanding at being able to formulate his message to the age group. He was a great leader and communicator. He took 13 and 14-year-olds from many different backgrounds and got them all on the same page. Boys want you to show them – and have less talk. Sure, Joe's really competent when it comes to baseball, but Joe was able to explain to the boys how to focus, be disciplined, the importance of why we practice stuff like pitcher's fielding practice and bunt coverages. You have to trust the process. Joe instilled confidence, kept enjoyment of the game, and made the kids realize that everyone's got some responsibility on every play.

Knowledge of the Game

Most people who become baseball coaches have a basic understanding of the game. Knowing the basic rules of the game is a must at every level. If you are the slightest bit unsure of game rules before the season, do some homework. Hopefully you can learn a lot from this book, but there are also countless other resources. It's critically important for you as a coach to continually be learning and growing so that you can become better at developing your players and teaching them the game.

Beyond the basic rules, a coach must understand the added modifications that come with playing in certain leagues, organizations, tournaments, and towns. For example, some tournaments may not allow a designated hitter or a courtesy runner for the catcher. Knowing what all of this means before games are played is imperative because you will need to be prepared for situations that may arise. Understanding these things will go a long way in maintaining your credibility with your players, parents, and opposing teams. And, you also want your players to have good experiences and be able to get playing time where possible.

Commitment

Once you decide to be a baseball coach, prepare to be "all in." This means that you have the time to do all the necessary things that go along with the job: preparation, understanding the game, scheduling, planning, practices and games, etc. Young ballplayers need coaches who are punctual and predictable. Seeing the same face and hearing the same voice over time will develop continuity for your players and organization. Be sure you are able to set aside the time it takes to do this job the right way. A few part time coaches who run teams may be well intended in sharing the responsibilities but are not usually effective in developing a consistent approach to teaching baseball.

Young players will naturally focus mainly on results. "I only went 1 for 4 today . . . it was a bad day." That's what usually sticks in a player's mind. It can be easy for them to forget that the team won or that they hit a couple hard line drives that happened to be right at fielders. As a coach, it is your job to keep players focused on the process and not the results. Kids need to be constantly reminded that perfection is not the goal, but rather improvement.

Story from Dan

Charlie, who works with me coaching some youth teams, is like Joe Girardi. He's excellent taking situations and keeping it in perspective. I remember clearly a really good 12-year old team that we had that was back fresh from a Cooperstown's tournament success on the 50-70 field. The team moved to the big/full size field in the fall at Baseball Heaven which is great preparation for the upcoming spring. I'll never forget losing to a team in the semi-finals – the kids were really down. Charlie said to the team after the game that the field doesn't get any bigger, but you do. What a great line! The boys were hitting balls well, but they weren't going anywhere because it was their first experience on the big field.

Chapter 3

Hitting

As long as baseball has been in existence there has been a fascination and wonder about hitting. Every young player I have ever had the good fortune to be around (and we are talking about *thousands*) has generally enjoyed fielding, throwing, and running the bases. But ALL of them LOVE to hit the ball. There is no better feeling in sport than squaring a ball up and watching it whistle off the bat.

Think of the iconic moments in the big leagues over the past 60 years or so – almost every one of them involves a hitter doing what we have all dreamed about doing ourselves: Bobby Thomson in the 1950's, Roger Maris in the 1960's, Reggie Jackson in the 1970's, Kirk Gibson in the 1980's, Joe Carter in the 1990's and yes, even "Mr. November", Derek Jeter, in this millennium. Launching a home run ball to help win your team a World Series title is the ultimate thrill in the great game of baseball.

However, this chapter is not designed to teach young players how to hit home runs or even give them a comprehensive analysis of the techniques involved in becoming a successful hitter. Instead, the goal simply is to begin to learn how to *think* about hitting and how to use the body to take effective swings. Another goal is to train the ballplayer's mind to realize that THINKING is for practice, and games are for REACTING.

If hitters have a deliberate focus on certain elements of their approach and swing during hitting sessions, this will lead to a higher level of consistency. The ultimate result is to begin to "feel" any differences in their game swings when the primary focus is to simply pick a good pitch to hit hard. I believe Mike Schmidt, Hall of Famer and the author of my favorite hitting book "The Mike Schmidt Study," captures the essence of this best: "As I look back, I would say my most important gift was 'feel.' I could always feel a good swing and log it into memory or alter it slightly with what I'd learned from trial-and-error and adjust from bad to good remarkably fast. I believe this ability came from plain swinging the bat continuously over many, many years. It's the combination of this feel, the experimentation and tinkering, and an infinite number of hours spent discussing hitting."

Ted Williams, arguably the greatest hitter of all time, once said, "I think without question the hardest single thing to do in sport is to hit a baseball." A hitter has mere tenths of a second to recognize and track the pitch in order to then either take the pitch or execute a swing. It is not possible to actively think in such a short amount of time – the body must react in the fashion that it has been trained and practiced. To develop a great hitting approach and swing, a tremendous amount of time and effort is required in order to prime the body to act and react in an optimal manner.

Always remember, there are no shortcuts! As many great players and coaches will tell you, the more you practice your swing, the better hitter you will be (within reasonable limits, of course, because overtraining can cause overuse injuries and burnout). What I want hitters to add to that equation is a smart work ethic and a deliberate focus on one or two elements of the swing at a time. Practice does not make PERFECT, it makes PERMANENT, and so let's make sure there is a purpose during every hitting session.

There is no one perfect swing or only one right way to hit; every individual is different and there is always room for interpretation and improvement. Set-up in the batter's box (stance), movements prior to the swing (commonly referred to as load, launch, trigger, gather, prep etc.), and the finish or follow through of the swing can all vary from hitter to hitter. However, the actions taken in *getting* to the contact point with the ball are somewhat similar in successful hitters. I believe coaches who are looking to make efficient and consistent improvements with their hitters do not teach from a cookie-cutter approach, but rather observe and analyze what each hitter's strengths and weaknesses might be and modify or adjust those areas specifically through drills and repetition.

⊘ ⊘ ⊘ ⊘ ⊘ ⊘ ⊘ **Story from Dan** ⊘ ⊘ ⊘ ⊘ ⊘ ⊘ ⊘

Some players try to be perfect. They tend to take too many swings in the batting cage until they are satisfied with their swing and hitting. I've had many kids that I've had to keep from overtraining – they end up ripping up their hands or injuring their lower back, etc. if they over practice. Their legs can get really sore (this is a tell-tale sign of excessive hitting). Kids get wrist injuries from just swinging too much. Players can start to change rhythm and tempo if they over practice. With fatigue, they may also tend to use the upper half of their body excessively.

Best example of someone who didn't overdo practice was former MLB outfielder Bernie Williams. He would stop after about 70 swings, but in a lesson, a kid might take 150 to 200 swings. It was shocking to me that Bernie would shut it down so quickly after after getting into a rhythm. I'm big on feel and comfort. It takes more reps for younger players to get to that level, but you don't want to go overboard.

Goal-Setting

When you ask a young baseball player what their goal is when they go up to bat, most will tell you it's to get a hit. That's a reasonable response considering the nature of the game. However, the reality is that no matter how talented they are, the likelihood of a player making an out is typically far higher than the likelihood of them getting a hit; failure is simply a substantial part of the game. Furthermore, whether or not they get a hit is something that, for the most part, a player has little control over. As a result, we need to revise our goals for hitters.

The goals of all hitters at any age level should be two-fold. The first goal is to have a quality at-bat. In order to understand and subsequently execute a quality at-bat, we first must recognize that what *defines* a quality at-bat will vary amongst different coaches and hitters. For the purposes of this book, here are a couple of simple examples:

Putting an aggressive swing on a pitch in a location where you know you can hit the ball hard.

Having a productive at-bat that helps your team get closer to scoring a run. This could mean working the count and having a ten-pitch at-bat, earning a walk, or hitting the ball to a certain part of the field to move runner(s) to the next base or to score them.

As you can see, there are certainly ways for a hitter to succeed in having a quality at-bat that do not always include getting a hit.

Second, hitters should strive to hit the ball hard. While this may seem less specific, no hitter can control whether or not they will get a base hit or a home run. If the hitter's mindset is to use the whole field and hit the ball hard, then they will increase their chance of being successful. Dwelling on batting average or the number of hits you had in your most recent game is a counterproductive approach bound to disappoint and frustrate. Even the best major league hitters on the planet are failing to get a hit about 70% of the time they go up to the plate! Baseball (hitting in particular) is a game of failure. These failures can be damaging to a player's self- confidence and can lead to poorer performances down the road. By redefining hitting success as having a quality at-bat or hitting the ball hard, we allow players to escape the trap of dwelling solely on the number of hits they had in the game. This mental shift ultimately frees players' minds and allows them to be the best player they can be in the long run.

Practice Preparation

The goal in hitting practice should be to develop a swing with repeatable, efficient mechanics. This is based upon a deliberate focus on certain elements the coach or player has defined as requiring specific attention. The more repetitions taken within this mindset, the easier it becomes to "feel" when something goes wrong. When something doesn't feel right, the players can make the appropriate adjustments to get back to the level of sustained consistency.

In hitting, I do not like to characterize swings as "good" or "bad" but rather "efficient" or "inefficient." Major league hitters might appear quite different on TV to fans (think about the violence of Bryce Harper's swing versus the smoothness of Mookie Betts's swing), but in reality, all good hitters try to be as efficient to the ball as possible. As mentioned earlier, a hitter has less than a second to recognize the speed, location, and type of pitch thrown to determine if they are going to swing or not. There is simply not enough time for wasted movement or inefficiency in the swing for a hitter to achieve the goal of consistently hitting the ball hard.

Game Preparation

Let's now create what I call *the anatomy of an at-bat*. During a game, when a hitter is on the bench they should be closely watching the opposing pitcher, focused on trying to pick up on any tendencies that could help them gain an advantage. It could be as simple as timing the speed of the pitch or figuring out that a pitcher speeds up his delivery to throw a fastball and slows his delivery down on an off-speed pitch. The pitcher might set his glove in a different spot before he winds up to throw a curveball, or he might lift his leg higher to generate more power for a fastball and not lift as high on an off-speed pitch. Discovering these "tells" or recognizing that a pitcher is "tipping" his pitches can be enormously helpful not just for the player as an individual, but also for the entire team if this information is effectively communicated.

When a hitter is "in the hole" (there are 2 hitters ahead of him) they should find an area to do any stretching or practice swinging. (Depending on the age group or field layout, this may not be possible. If this is the case, then a player can simply stretch in the dugout or bench area). This is the time when players really begin to prepare their bodies to execute their plan when they get into the batter's box.

When a hitter is "on-deck" (hitting next), they should incorporate both relaxation and timing. Everything players do on the baseball field should be done with the body relaxed (without tension). If a player wants to create bat speed and a quick, efficient path to the baseball, they must be loose and comfortable.

Two specific things that I recommend hitters do in the on-deck circle are to breathe deeply (in order to keep the heart rate down and stay calm), and to visualize their upcoming at-bat. During this down time in the on-deck circle, players can visualize themselves in the batter's box tracking the ball out of the pitcher's hand and taking a quality swing that results in a line drive. After the player has visualized hitting the ball hard, they can get into their stance, and time the delivery of the pitcher as if they were in the batter's box. Hitters should work on the technique of putting an imaginary small box around the hand of the pitcher's release point. This will allow them to pick up the ball as early as possible. Remember, the longer a hitter sees the ball, the greater the chance they have to be on time and hit the ball hard.

As a hitter approaches the plate for their turn to hit, they can create what Mike Schmidt calls, "one positive thought" in their mind. For example, "I'm going to smack a line drive right up the middle." No matter how well the opposing pitcher is pitching, or how poorly a hitter has been swinging the bat on that particular day, or how big the situation is, a hitter should ALWAYS expect to hit the ball hard. If a hitter goes to the plate thinking things like, "I stink" or "I'm gonna strike out again," it will only increase the likelihood of them fulfilling these low expectations.

During an at-bat, frustration or negativity will often creep into a hitter's mind. The hitter might bemoan a bad call made by the umpire or wish they could have another swing at a fastball that they just missed and fouled straight back. When these thoughts start to creep into a player's mind, he should ask for time and step out of the batter's box. He should take a deep breath, allow time to reset, and erase the negative thoughts clouding his mind and recall his "one positive thought" for the at-bat.

Again, practice habits can't be overstated. Extensive preparation will allow hitters to feel more comfortable and confident going into at-bats. It's easy for players to say to themselves, "be confident" or "stay positive," but quite another for them to actually believe it and have their swing back it up. The best advice you can give your player is to remind them that they've done it plenty of times before in practice, and that they are prepared . . . not only *can* they have a quality at-bat, but they *will* have a quality at-bat.

Stance and Pre-Swing Rhythm

There are a variety of stances employed by successful hitters, which indicates that there are numerous ways to begin the process of swinging a baseball bat. However, there are certain guidelines that I believe all young hitters should follow:

Be Loose and Relaxed. Each hitter should have a stance that allows their body to be relaxed and their hands to be loose. They should also create some sort of controlled movement or rhythm so that they do not become tense or stiff before the pitch is delivered.

Complete Plate Coverage. Each hitter should find a place in the batter's box where they feel confident that they can cover the outside half of the plate with the barrel of the bat, but not so close to the plate that a pitch on the inside corner ends up jamming them or gets pulled foul.

Be Positioned to See the Ball Well. The most important aspect of hitting is vision. You can't hit well what you can't see well. The simplest way to obtain optimal vision is to have the chin above the front shoulder so both eyes have a clear, unimpeded view of the pitcher's release point. Any stance or pre-pitch action that obscures the pitcher from the hitter's line of vision needs to be avoided.

Swing Mechanics

There are many different philosophies for teaching and learning swing mechanics. Players need to find the style and approach that feels most comfortable to them and *always keep it simple*. It can be confusing and frustrating for a young hitter to have multiple coaches teaching them different (and sometimes conflicting) ways to swing the bat. It is always best to keep the message clear and concise using consistent language to relay the information. *Hitting a baseball is a reactionary function that has been mastered by very few.* To overanalyze the movements or clutter the brain with a variety of thoughts will make it nearly impossible for a hitter to achieve sustainable success. The following information speaks in general terms and can easily be adjusted or adapted based on the skill level, athleticism, strength, progress and comfort of each hitter.

Beginning with the lower half of the body, I generally like to see a hitter set up in the following manner (see picture 3-1):

3-1: Set up in a comfortable athletic stance, square to home plate and in line with the pitcher.

- ⊘ The feet about a bat length apart

- ⊘ The feet in line with the pitcher

- ⊘ The body square to the plate

- ⊘ The knees bent comfortably in an athletic stance

In order to get kids in the proper hitting position, it can be helpful to ask them, "how would you guard someone in basketball," or "how would you field a ground ball?" Many times, the hitter will get themselves into a good hitting position in response to these cues because it allows them to be athletic and create a strong foundation or base from which to begin the swing.

A common flaw I see with young hitters is setting up with their feet too far apart from each other (see picture 3-2). This restricts the use of rotational forces in the hips causing the arms to do the majority of the work in the swing mechanics.

3-2: Setting up with your feet too far apart can prevent you from using your hips properly during the swing

In contrast, some young hitters like to set up in an "open" stance (see picture 3-3)—front foot is further from the plate than is the back foot—and/or "small" (see picture 3-4)—feet less than a bat length apart. These stances can sometimes contribute to issues in timing and stride direction. However, being "open" and/or "small" in the stance

3-3: In an open stance, the front foot is further from the plate than the back foot.

3-4: Setting up "small" with the feet too close together can lead to swing issues.

can work for a hitter as long as they are aware that they must create a strong, athletic base once the ball is in flight and the front foot action is completed by being on the ground.

The upper half of the hitter's body should likewise be square to the plate with the shoulders either in a straight line or slightly closed off to the pitcher. This allows the entire body to work together efficiently and comfortably throughout the swing sequence.

Coaches often overlook the way in which a young player grips a base-ball bat. Many assume that it's just "natural" that a player knows how to do it. However, I've seen lots of players who over or under-rotate their hands, or who hold the bat too tightly. These all lead to diffi-cult, unnatural, and uncomfortable swings. With the grip, the bat

3-5: A strong, comfortable grip should have the bat held loosely at the base of the fingers.

3-6: Under-rotating the hands may cause the player to have a weak grip on the bat.

should be held loosely at the base of the fingers (see pictures 3-5, 3-6 and 3-7). Some hitters will have the bat deep in their palms, which, in my opinion, often decreases the "whipping" action of the barrel in the hitting zone. The grip must be comfortable and give the hitter the ability to control their movements to the ball in a consistent, short,

3-7: Over-rotating the hands may cause the player to hold the bat too deep in their palms.

quick manner. Usually, the hitter's grip becomes firmer when the front foot lands in the launch position, preparing for these movements to the ball.

The initial placement of the hitter's hands varies, but a safe position to start from is with the hands at the top and off the back of the shoulder, and a comfortable distance away from the body. The bat head is typically positioned between the top of the back shoulder and the head, with the angle of the bat pointed slightly towards the ear (see picture 3-8).

3-8: The hitter's hands should be just off the back shoulder with the bat head positioned between the top of the back shoulder and the head.

Before and as a pitch is thrown, many young hitters will move their bodies in all sorts of ways to get their swings started. Some wiggle their bats around, some shift their weight between their legs, and some won't move at all! All pre-swing movements with the body should be under control. As the front foot begins to leave the ground, every hitter's actions should be relaxed and fluid, and the weight should begin to transfer to the back side.

Remember, something must go back before going forward. As this shift occurs, the hitter should begin to feel strong on the inside part of the back leg. At the same time, the hands should remain loose and begin a controlled, subtle "push back" or trace a small backwards "C" to a strong launch position. The front foot movement, weight distribution and hand adjustment should all work together in a rhythmic, controlled, balanced, and fluid action.

The front foot landing should be short, straight, soft and closed. Over-striding will often cause the hitter to have trouble timing up the pitch. Landing should be in a straight line toward the pitcher, not toward first base or third base which can create poor angles to the hitting zone. Landing hard or fast will rush the weight shift and drag the barrel through the hitting zone. If the front foot is too open as it lands, the front hip and shoulder action will occur too soon. This results in a swing that is slower and longer to the hitting zone causing loss of power and plate coverage.

The front leg should be strong and firm allowing the hitter to begin hip rotation in an aggressive manner. The "explosion" or "drive" of the lower half is directly connected to using the front leg as a "brace" to absorb the rotational forces of the hips. If the front leg lands too stiff, it will cause the front hip and shoulder to "pull off" early, creating a long bat path to the ball. If the front leg has too much flexion and the weight shifts too heavily to the front side, the hitter will "collapse" in the lower half, causing the bat to drag and the head to move an excessive distance.

The aggressive, powerful rotation of the hips will initiate the hands and bat to the hitting zone in a "tight" and efficient manner. The longer the hands can remain in a good launch position and *follow* the hip rotation, the more bat speed and "level" plane can be created to the contact point with the ball. When the hands or the front side do too much work early in the process, we miss out on much of the power that is generated from the separation between the earlier rotation of the hips and the lower half of the body, and subsequent rotation of the upper half of the body.

At contact with the ball, the hands should be "tight" to the body and in a "palm up, palm down" position, which means that the top hand palm should be facing the sky while the bottom hand palm is facing the ground (see picture 3-9). The top arm should be in an "L" shape, the hitter's eyes should be focused on the ball and the back knee should be bent. From here, the extension phase begins. The barrel continues through the hitting zone as the arms fully extend out in front creating the effect of "looking down the barrel of the bat." At this point, the top hand palm begins to turn over and the finishing (or follow through) phase begins. If the swing is level and efficient, the hitter maximizes bat speed,

3-9: Getting to a good, strong palm-up, palm-down position at contact should put the hitter in the right place to extend through the baseball.

power, and the ability to make contact with the pitch. When all of the pieces are put together, a hitting approach and swing should look fluid, natural, rhythmic, and under control—not mechanical and forced.

Bunting

Bunting is one of the least taught, underused offensive weapons at every level of the game. This skill requires very little natural ability other than some hand-eye coordination. *The ability to learn to bunt is a mindset.* If a player has the desire and determination to practice the techniques, they will become a good bunter and a more valuable player to the team and coaches. At some point, even the best hitters might be asked to sacrifice bunt. And, especially if a player has good speed, they can bunt for base hits.

Here are some general guidelines to follow when practicing the *sacrifice* bunt (used to move base runners while conceding an out):

⊘ The hitter moves up slightly from their regular set-up to the front part of the batter's box.

⊘ Pivots both feet in place so that the toes on the back foot are pointed towards the pitcher.

⊘ The upper body rotates in order to be square to the pitcher.

⊘ The knees should be bent creating an athletic stance, with weight slightly forward (see picture 3-10).

⊘ The bat is gripped loosely, with the bottom hand staying near the knob and the top hand sliding up

3-10: When bunting, the hitter should pivot their feet so that their toes and upper body are square to the pitcher, with their knees bent in an athletic stance.

towards the label of the bat (see picture 3-11).

⊘ The barrel of the bat should initially be positioned at the top of the strike zone and angled slightly upwards, with the barrel higher than the handle.

⊘ The hands and bat are out in front of the body in order to "catch" the ball with the bat by "giving" or "pulling back" with both hands as the ball makes contact.

⊘ To bunt towards first or third base, the bottom hand shifts slightly to adjust the angle of the barrel creating a bat angle toward the desired bunt direction.

3-11: The bat should be gripped loosely with the bottom hand staying near the knob, the top hand sliding up towards the label, and the barrel of the bat slightly above the handle.

Lastly, it is important to remember to always keep the barrel of the bat above the knob, if the barrel falls below the knob, the bunt will be missed, popped up, or fouled off.

When bunting for a base hit, hitters should "show" bunt, or "square around" to bunt much later in the pitcher's windup. While sacrifice bunters are typically taught to show bunt when the pitcher starts their windup or gets to their balance point, a hitter bunting for a base hit should wait as late as they can to show bunt – possibly after the pitcher breaks their hands separating the ball from his glove – to maintain the element of surprise. A hitter's goal here is to get on base. As opposed to a sacrifice bunt, hitters bunting for a hit should try to place their bunt closer to the first or third base line (it helps to aim at the actual fielders playing those positions rather than the baseline).

Summary

1. Keep it simple. Don't try to do too much in the approach, either mentally or physically.

2. Less is more. Do not exaggerate movement. The more moving parts there are for young hitters, the tougher it is to repeat.

3. There's no such thing as a right or wrong swing but an efficient or inefficient swing. (Hitting philosophy-positive reinforcement).

4. Preparation breeds confidence. Believe in yourself and abilities based on hard work, deliberate focus and sound practice habits.

5. Hitters should know they don't have to swing "hard" in order to hit the ball hard. You want to be aggressive but under control and allow the transference of energy to occur from lower half (explosion) to upper half (bat speed) through efficient body movements.

6. The best hitters use the big part of the field which is the alley from over the shortstop's head to over the second baseman's head.

7. Practice is for thinking, games are for reacting.

8. Create athleticism and some rhythm in the stance/set-up.

9. Maximize bat speed by remaining tension-free from set-up throughout the swing sequence.

10. Make it your goal to hit line drives.

Chapter 4

Pitching

Many baseball coaches agree that good pitching beats good hitting. In fact, nearly all successful teams at the youth, college and professional level have quality defenses that make the routine plays and a solid pitching staff. While a team might have a lineup full of players who hit the ball extremely well, they may not win many games if their pitchers give up too many runs. Giving up too many walks, hit batters and hits usually leads to problems. This is why pitching is one of most important aspects of baseball.

⊘ ⊘ ⊘ ⊘ ⊘ ⊘ ⊘ **Story from Dan** ⊘ ⊘ ⊘ ⊘ ⊘ ⊘ ⊘
Game Pitchers Should Earn Their Stripes in Practice

At the younger age levels, some coaches will give every player on the team an opportunity to pitch. This can lead to some horribly boring "walk-athons" where some pitchers walk batter after batter. Just as you shouldn't put a player at first base who can't catch, I don't think it's in anyone's interest to put young players on the mound who can't throw strikes.

I strongly suggest that coaches use practice time to teach interested players how to pitch and then allow players who can throw a reasonable percent-age of strikes (at least 33%, ideally 50%) in a practice situation to pitch in games. With the added stress of fans, parents, umpires and opposing players and coaches, it's generally harder for kids to throw strikes in a game situation than it is in practice. While it is important to give young ballplayers the ability to play a variety of different positions, it simply is not in anyone's best interests to put a young player on the mound who is not capable of throwing a reasonable portion of strikes in a game situation.

At the youth level, throwing strikes and having good rhythm and tempo on the mound are critically important. By working efficiently and consistently throwing strikes, pitchers help keep their fielders engaged in the game and give themselves and their team a better chance to succeed. Moreover, in this day and age of increased emphasis on pitch counts, throwing strikes and being effective allows a pitcher to stay in the game longer.

Pitching Mechanics

Just like a good swing, the way in which a pitcher throws should be a motion that is easily repeatable. Coaches should take note of four basic things when evaluating or working with a young pitcher:

1. Whether or not the pitcher is consistently throwing strikes

2. The pitcher's velocity

3. Movement on the pitcher's ball

4. Mechanics: including arm action, consistency of release point, arm slot and use of the lower half in the delivery

Sometimes a good young pitcher will be able to pound the strike zone, throw the ball hard and get quality movement on his pitches with a motion that may appear unorthodox or herky-jerky. This is acceptable as long as the pitcher is not experiencing pain or putting himself at greater risk of an injury. Just like there might not be just one way to solve a problem, there are many different ways in which a pitcher can succeed; while a smoother, more conventional motion might work for one pitcher, another pitcher might rely upon a more unorthodox delivery to achieve a level of consistency and get batters out. Not all good pitchers have to look exactly alike in their mechanics and delivery.

33

A pitcher's goal is to try and keep hitters off balance and there are numerous different ways to do this. Many of the best pitchers are deceptive. Perhaps their changeup looks just like a fastball coming out of their hand, or maybe they hide the ball really well up until they release a pitch. Regardless, pitchers (and their coaches) should continue learning about and experimenting with ways to become more effective whether it be in the form of increased velocity, more movement on pitches or even a more deceptive delivery.

Starting Position

Pitching can be broken down into four main phases:

1. Starting (or Set) Position (Pictures 4-1, 4-2)

4-1: Example of the starting (set) position

4-2: Example of the stretch position position

2. Balance Position (Picture 4-3)

3. Power Position (Picture 4-4)

4-3: The balance position   4-4: The power position

4. Release and Follow Through (Picture 4-5, 4-6)

In order to begin working with a young pitcher, coaches should first take a look at his starting position. With no runners on base, pitchers should start from a full wind-up with their feet between six inches and shoulder width apart on top of the rubber (see picture 4-1). The hands should be held at either the waist or chest and the body should be relaxed. Where exactly the pitcher stands on the rubber is ultimately a matter of preference. A pitcher should stand in the place where they feel the most comfortable and are best at throwing strikes from. For some pitchers, this might be on the third base side of the rubber while

4-5: Release and follow through   4-6: Release and follow through

for others it might be closer towards first base. A good starting point for most young pitchers though, should be in the center of the rubber.

When working from the stretch (with runners on base), the pitcher should begin with his feet slightly wider than shoulder width apart looking in at the sign from his catcher. (Pitchers use this method to be able to better hold runners on base, simplify mechanics, deliver the ball more quickly, and to prevent easy stolen bases.) After receiving the sign, the pitcher should come to the set position with his feet about shoulder width apart and the hands together at the waist or chest (see picture 4-2). Again, the body should be relaxed; pitchers can gather themselves by taking a deep breath before beginning their delivery.

When starting from the wind-up (no runners on base), pitchers should set up with their feet approximately shoulder width apart with their hands held at their waist or chest (see picture 4-1).

When pitching from the stretch position, after receiving the sign, the pitcher should come to the set position (with runners on base) with their feet shoulder width apart and the hands held at their waist or chest (see picture 4-2).

For young pitchers who are having trouble throwing strikes, try having them eliminate the windup from their motion and pitch exclusively from the stretch. This can help simplify things, keep their motion "quiet" and may help young pitchers avoid the problem of having too many things to think about at once.

Balance Position

In order to begin the pitching motion from the windup, the pitcher should take a small step back and to the side with the glove side foot—pitching from the stretch eliminates this step (see picture 4-7). This first step should be comfortable and not rushed. Encourage your pitchers not to use an exaggerated weight shift here (see pictures 4-8, 4-9). Their weight should be centered over the pitching rubber at all times during this movement. The throwing side foot then pivots and presses against the front side of the rubber before the glove side leg drives up to the chest causing the front knee to come up to parallel with the front hip (see picture 4-10). The front foot

4-7: To initiate the pitching motion from the windup, the pitcher should take a small step back and to the side with the glove side foot, keeping their weight centered over the rubber

37

4-8: Stepping too far back can cause the pitcher to lose his balance

4-9: Stepping too far to the side can cause the pitcher to lose his balance

should be relaxed with the toe pointed towards the ground and the back leg should be slightly bent to maintain balance.

Throughout these movements, it's critical that the pitcher maintains his balance and rhythm at all times—he should keep his eyes up and focused on the target. A pitcher who is constantly off-balance when delivering the baseball will certainly not be able to repeat the motion and throw strikes consistently.

Power Position

Getting the pitcher into a proper power position is crucial in maximizing velocity and regularly throwing strikes. To help keep your

4-10: The throwing side foot then pivots and presses against the front side of the rubber, before the glove side leg drives up to the chest bringing the pitcher to a balance position

4-11: "As the front leg drops down and slides forward, the hands should separate with both thumbs down the ground bringing the pitcher to a strong power position"

front side stay closed, pitching instructors recommend that you keep your pitching hand back and trailing or following your lower half toward home plate. As the front leg drops down and slides forward, the hands should separate with both thumbs down to the ground. A common mistake for young pitchers is "reaching" with the front foot without pushing off the rubber with their back leg. This results in a loss of velocity and lot of added stress to the pitcher's arm. During the stride, it's critical that pitchers remember down *and then* out—separation of the hands should should occur as the front leg begins to lower from the highest point of the balance position. This will ensure that they are using their back leg properly to push off the rubber.

When the front foot lands, it should be slightly closed (for a righty, pointed towards the right-handed batters box and for a lefty, towards the left-handed batters box) and in a straight line with the back foot and home plate (see picture 4-11). The throwing arm ideally should be bent at the elbow creating an "L" shape with the throwing elbow above the throwing shoulder, with the wrist relaxed. That said, not all good pitchers do this or do it all of the time—they may have less of an angle and throw from different "arm slots." This is fine so long as they have good posture, can consistently throw strikes and keep their arm and shoulder in good health.

4-12: As the pitcher releases the ball, it should "snap" off his fingertips with backspin rotation. His back leg will then rotate around leaving him a strong fielding position

From a coaching standpoint, it's important to ensure that your pitchers are not allowing their elbow to drop below their shoulder as they rotate to throw. When a pitcher's elbow drops too low, he may tend to have the ball sail on him. Furthermore, this can contribute to a loss in velocity and to an increased risk of injury.

Release and Follow Through

As the pitcher releases the ball, it should "snap" off his fingertips with backspin rotation (see picture 4-12). Keep in mind that his fingertips should be above and behind the baseball during this stage. This part of the pitching motion is a result of the momentum the pitcher has created throughout the first three phases of the pitch up until this point.

The throwing arm should extend out then towards the ground as the back leg stays on the ground until the ball is released before coming over and landing parallel to the front leg. The pitcher should land in an athletic position with feet about shoulder width apart, ready to make a play on a ball hit back at the mound (see picture 4-13). After releasing the ball, pitchers are fielders and should be ready to cover first base on balls hit to the right side that require the first baseman to field. Pitchers also have other responsibilities

4-13: As the pitcher releases the ball, it should "snap" off his fingertips with backspin rotation. His back leg will then rotate around leaving him a strong fielding position

such as backing up throws to third and home and possibly being involved in relays on the smaller field.

Pitch Selection

My pitching philosophy for young kids is simple. Develop your fastball and learn to and work at locating it (hitting the catcher's target). Many young baseball pitchers (and some coaches) become enamored with throwing curveballs and sliders, but the reality is that throwing breaking balls too soon is simply not in their best interests in terms of their long-term development as athletes and ballplayers. Kids should not begin throwing breaking balls until they enter high school. At 11 and 12 years of age, their arms are simply not ready, and they risk injuries to their arms. Just look at the number of kids that young these days getting costly and complicated Tommy John surgery!

Furthermore, the more fastballs they throw, the more arm strength kids are going to build. All young kids want to throw harder and the best way to develop a good fastball is by throwing more of them.

4-14: Four-seam fastball grip

4-15: Two-seam fastball grip

Pitchers should also learn to locate their fastball to both sides of the plate. When a young pitcher has good control with his four-seam fastball (see picture 4-14), he can experiment with a two-seam fastball in order to get some movement (see picture 4-15). A good two seam fastball thrown by a righty can run in on the hands of a right-handed hitter and dive down and away from a lefty. Even professional pitchers with less than stellar velocity can succeed if they can hit their spots, work the "black" (sides of the plate) and keep the hitters off balance. If it works for major leaguers, it certainly can work for little leaguers too.

Once a young pitcher has developed good command of his fastball, he should begin working on a good changeup. This puts much less stress on a kid's arm than a curveball and is also an effective off-speed pitch. One way to grip the changeup is by starting with a four-seam grip and then taking the ring finger and putting it across the seams with the pointer and middle fingers. The ball is held in the same way that a fastball is held but will come out of the hand slower. A pitcher's arm speed should be the same when throwing a change-up as it is when throwing a fastball. This will allow pitchers to deceive hitters into gearing up for a fastball when in reality, a slower pitch is on its way to home plate.

4-16: Circle changeup grip

4-17: Circle changeup grip

Another common way to hold a changeup is by making a circle with the thumb and index finger to cradle the ball, with the remaining three fingers placed across the seams—think about making an "OK" sign with the fingers (see picture 4-16, 4-17). This is generally more effective for kids whose hands are a little larger. It's important to remember that however a player chooses to hold the baseball, a good change-up should look just like a fastball coming out of the pitcher's hand, and that this is accomplished by throwing the changeup with the same arm speed and motion that is used in throwing a fastball.

One final and important point on gripping change-ups versus fastballs. With a fastball, the grip is more with the finger tips whereas a change-up is gripped deeper in the hand.

Minimizing Injuries

Coaches should be careful about overusing their pitchers. Kids can get injured due to overuse and/or bad mechanics. Dr. James Andrews, an orthopedic surgeon famous for performing surgery on numerous pitchers with arm injuries, says that he used to perform Tommy John surgery on three or four high school athletes a year. Today, he says, maybe three or four young pitchers are coming in for surgery *each week*.

So, what can coaches do to prevent this? For starters, make sure that young kids are not throwing too much and also are not throwing too many breaking balls. One thing that is many times overlooked is how a pitcher gets to a certain pitch count. A pitcher who is cruising and consistently throwing 12 or 15 pitches an inning might not be as tired at 75 pitches as a kid who just went out and threw a 30-pitch inning. Don't mindlessly follow pitch counts—if player has a really long inning (e.g. 30+ pitches) in the fourth inning, you should watch him closely if you're going to send him out to pitch the fifth inning. Going through a long inning places much more stress and strain on a pitcher. Use common sense and an "eye test"—consider velocity if it's gone down, consistency in the zone, etc. Signs of fatigue can include losing push in the legs or "short-arming" (not fully extending your arm) the ball. Furthermore, while one kid might be laboring to maintain good mechanics at 65 pitches, another kid might look like he just started the game. All these factors must be taken into consideration when coaches are discussing fatigue, pitch count and overuse.

Also, kids should not be throwing seven days a week and should be mindful of how many throws they are making on a daily basis. Taking a couple of days off per week from throwing is a good goal to aim for. Cal Ripken, USA Baseball, Little League and most other youth baseball leagues now have required days off from pitching after throwing a certain number of pitches. The table below summarizes typical rest requirements from pitching. Young pitchers should get used to the idea of doing very little throwing or no throwing at all the day after a long outing on the mound.

Age	Daily Max (Pitches)	Required Rest (Pitches)				
		0 Days	1 Day	2 Days	3 Days	4 Days
7–8	50	1–20	21–35	36–50	N/A	N/A
9–10	75	1–20	21–35	36–50	51–65	66+
11–12	85	1–20	21–35	36–50	51–65	66+
13–14	95	1–20	21–35	36–50	51–65	66+
15–16	95	1–30	31–45	46–60	61–75	76+
17–18	105	1–30	31–45	46–60	61–75	76+

Source: MLB/USA Baseball

The best advice I can give is to always err on the side of caution. Winning or losing a game at ten or twelve years old is certainly not worth risking a kid's health and future. If a coach at the youth level is prioritizing winning a tournament over player development or arm health, he needs to get his priorities straight.

Chapter 5

Infielding

I t's the bottom of the last inning, and the home team is clinging to a one-run lead. There are two outs, and the tying run is on third. The batter hits the ball sharply on the ground into the hole between short and third . . . the shortstop goes full speed, stretches way out and fields the ball backhanded . . . sets and throws to first . . . the first baseman stretches and catches the ball just before the runner reaches the base . . . OUT!

Baseball fans young and old appreciate the beauty of watching an infielder make a sparkling play to take a hit away from the batter. When watching major league highlights, I sometimes find myself in awe seeing what the best infielders can do on the diamond. In this chapter I'll break down some of the essential points of being an infielder: positioning, fielding form, footwork, and position specific skills.

Preparation: Finding the Proper Glove

It's common to see youth baseball players using gloves that are either too big or too small for their hands. (In fact, a college teammate of mine unknowingly used an outfielder's glove for two seasons while playing shortstop before he learned he could've been using a much smaller glove!) Middle infielders should try to use smaller, lighter gloves in order to facilitate quick transfers between the glove and their throwing hand. Third basemen will use a slightly larger glove, while first basemen will use a larger, specially made glove that gives them a wider surface to catch the ball with. As long as a player is having success in the field, though, kids should use whatever feels most comfortable to them.

Preparation: Pre-Pitch Routine

Infielders should always prepare for each pitch in a *quality defensive ready position*. This means being in an athletic stance on the balls of their feet with their knees comfortably bent. The glove and throwing hands should be relaxed and out in front of the body (see picture 5-1). In order to create rhythm and stay relaxed, infielders should have some sort of pre-pitch motion. I recommend that players take "creeper" steps (small steps forward) as the ball is delivered to home plate. This will keep them in motion and ready to move quickly to wherever the ball is hit. I often see young players planted on their heels pitch after pitch. That's fine . . . unless the ball is hit toward them!

Here's another way to think about being ready. Taking a page from tennis—watch tennis players getting ready to receive a fast serve. They take a step in and a hop to be ready to react.

5-1: An athletic defensive ready position

◉ ◉ ◉ ◉ ◉ ◉ ◉ *Story from Dan* ◉ ◉ ◉ ◉ ◉ ◉ ◉

After I was drafted by the Los Angeles Dodgers, the first thing I received when I reported to my minor league team was the "Dodger manual." It emphasized that you prepare yourself to be doing something on every play. Sure, younger players may feel bored and that they may not get the ball on the next play, but they should be *doing* something on every play. The first page of the Dodger's manual was what to do on a routine ground ball with no one on base. There were arrows showing what all the players on the field should be doing. Everyone has a responsibility and should be moving – this is greatly underappreciated and under taught. Too many players feel like they have nothing to do if the ball isn't coming at them. A lot of this is common sense – for example, outfielders backing up ground balls hit to an infielder, the right fielder running toward the foul line on a throw to first base.

Fielding Form - Ground Balls

In terms of actually fielding a ground ball, infielders need to create a wide base, get their butt down, and field the ball with their hands out in front of their body (see picture 5-2). Having a wide base allows them to get their backside down which automatically shifts their weight out in front where their hands should be when fielding the ball (see picture 5-3 for the common mistake of the fielder's base being too narrow). Many coaches call this set up a "Fielder's Triangle" with the infielder's

5-2: Good wide base, fielding the ball in front of his body

two feet and glove forming the three points of the triangle. The ball should be fielded at the "top" of the triangle, which is part of the triangle closest to home plate. (As players advance, they will begin playing the ball toward the inside foot—left foot for right-handed throwers—in order to get into throwing position more quickly.)

A common mistake for young infielders is letting the ball get too deep and trying to field it back between their legs (see picture 5-4). This makes it more difficult for them to track the ball into their glove, and also puts them in a poor position to

5-3: Common mistake: a base that is too narrow

react to bad hops. By fielding ground balls out in front of the body, infielders can give themselves a much better chance to readjust in order to catch or block a ball that takes a bad or erratic hop (see picture 5-5).

On a routine ground ball, infielders should use both hands: using the glove hand to receive the ball, and the throwing hand to transfer the ball quickly out of the glove into a throwing position. Once the ball is caught, the player must quickly get the ball to a teammate (most likely at one of the bases). Here is the sequence infielders should follow to efficiently finish the play once they've secured a ground ball:

Ⓢ Shuffle feet toward the *target* (where they want to throw the ball). This creates efficient momentum to make a strong, accurate throw.

5-4: Common mistake: Fielding the ball between the player's legs rather than out on front of the body

5-5: Fielding the ball properly, out in front of the body

⊘ At the same time, the player's upper-half of the body shifts into "power" (throwing) position.

⊘ The throwing side foot should "replace" (step into the vacated position) the glove side foot, to again create momentum toward the target (see picture 5-6).

⊘ The glove side foot *closes* the front side toward wherever the fielder is throwing to (see picture 5-7).

⊘ The front side of the body (foot, hip, shoulder and elbow) should be lined up with the target before the throwing arm begins to come forward.

5-6: *Throwing side foot replaces the glove side foot*

5-7: Glove side foot closes the front side towards the target

✪ As the ball moves forward toward the release point, the torso rotates with the glove side "pulling" the throwing side through (see picture 5-8).

✪ After the ball is released, the throwing arm extends out to the target and the body's momentum continues moving forward in the follow through phase.

5-8: The ball is released, and the body's momentum continues moving forward towards the target

On routine plays, a ¾ arm slot should be used as a general rule of thumb—plays made deep in the hole or moving away from the target generally require the infielder to throw more "over the top." When making these longer throws, the throwing side elbow should be in line with the shoulder, and not below it.

Every throw made by an infielder should be made using a four-seam grip on the baseball (see the pitching chapter for a more detailed discussion on grips). This helps ensure that the ball will fly straight and also *carry* (travel the expected distance) as a normal throw should. A ball that dips and dives on its way to the first baseman will only make his job more difficult and will likely result in more errors.

Infielders should also get used to aiming for a specific point on the target's body or glove (if a good target is consistently created), instead of just the first baseman in general. By aiming for the target player's glove, chest or head/cap, it allows infielders to narrow their focus and will encourage them to throw the ball where it will be easiest for their teammate to make the catch; in other words, it minimizes the chances for a throwing error or an error by the first baseman.

First Base

First base is arguably the most unusual of the four infield positions. Many first-basemen are left handed, while the other infield positions are generally righties. First basemen don't necessarily have to be fast but should be quick to react to situations. Finally, first basemen are involved in many infield plays, and must be good at receiving and catching the ball.

There are two essential things for young first basemen to remember. First, if the ball is not hit to them and there's going to be a play at first base, they need to quickly get to the base in order to set their bodies up and give a good target. Second, they should remember to stretch toward the baseball as it is in the air.

At the youth level, the primary responsibility of a first baseman is going to be receiving throws from other infielders. As a result, the younger the age group, the closer to the bag your first baseman should probably be setting up in their defensive position.

When a ground ball is hit to any other infielder, the first baseman needs to get to the bag early and set up to give a good target. He should be standing tall rather than crouching and should not be moving when the thrower is ready to throw the ball. The goal should be to give the other infielders a big, wide target to throw to.

In terms of footwork, first basemen should set up with the heel of the throwing side foot in the center of the inside part of the bag—e.g., a left-hander will set up with his left foot touching the inside of the base and a right hander with his right foot touching the inside of the base (see picture 5-9). Placing the foot directly on top of the base puts players at risk of being stepped on by the runner, and also pulls them further away from their fielders. Once the throw is made, the glove and glove side foot should work together to catch the ball. Ideally, the ball should hit the player's glove at the same time the glove-side foot hits the ground (see pictures 5-10, 5-11).

5-9: *First Basemen should set up with the heel of the throwing side foot in the center of the inside part of the bag*

5-10: Once the throw is made, the glove and glove side foot should work together to catch the ball

Third Base

The third baseman plays relatively close to the hitter (much closer than the middle infielders). Thus, third basemen should hold their glove closer to the ground in the ready position to react more quickly to balls. Positioning in general is a crucial element of a third baseman's role. With such a short reaction time, this pre-pitch decision can make or break their ability to turn a hard two-hopper or line drive into an out. All other things considered, normal positioning will be deep and off the third base line—probably 5 or 6 steps behind the bag and 3 or 4 steps away from it.

Double play depth for a third baseman means taking a few steps closer to the plate and a few towards second base from where normal depth

is so that there will be enough time to attempt to turn a double play on hard hit balls. This also might be where it's necessary to play for hitters that run well. In potential bunt situations, a third baseman should step up at least to the edge of the grass on the infield and probably a step or two closer if it's an obvious sacrifice situation. If the hitter squares and shows bunt early, then they can charge and cut down on that space even more.

5-11: Once the throw is made, the glove and glove side foot should work together to catch the ball

Middle Infield

In youth baseball and at the big-league level, the middle infielders (the second baseman and the shortstop) are generally good athletes. They need to have good range and be quick enough to get to balls hit in the hole (between the third baseman and shortstop or between the first baseman and second baseman) and up the middle. Good middle infielders have quick hands, ball transfer skills, and strong and accurate throwing arms. While fielding ground balls and throwing runners out at first is a top priority of these two middle infield positions, these players must regularly work in tandem to help their team succeed on defense.

Double Play Situations

No matter how athletic they might be, shortstops and second base-men need to position themselves closer to second base in a possible double play situation. When a middle infielder approaches second base to receive the ball and potentially throw the ball to first, it is called a "pivot" play.

Ideally, the second baseman and shortstop should get themselves in a position so that they can get to second base and set up to be a good target on a sharply hit ball to the infield. If a shortstop is consistently catching the ball on a dead sprint from another infielder, they are prob-ably setting up too far from the bag.

A coach might instruct fielders to play at "double play depth." This is usually the furthest point from which a middle infielder can make an underhand "flip" to the second base bag. This spot, or "comfort zone" varies from player to player. A middle infielder that is a step slower than most might need to set up a little closer to second base, while

5-12: To turn a double play, the second baseman should set up with their left foot on the bag, and their shoulders square to their teammate

5-13: On a throw right to their chest, a second baseman can take their right foot across the bag towards third base before planting and throwing

a quicker player might be able to play a step or two further from the base. Experience will help players at any level to recognize their optimal double play depth. Regardless, a middle infielder should play in a position where they can comfortably and reliably get to the bag and not rush the throw in order to turn a double play.

For second basemen receiving the throw, the first thing they need to do is get to the bag early, set up with their left foot on the bag and get their shoulders square to the thrower—usually the shortstop or the third baseman (see picture 5-12). From here there are three simple ways a second baseman can turn a double play at second. On a throw that's right on line toward them, they can step straight toward the ball with the right foot (moving across the bag towards third base), plant and throw (see pictures 5-13, 5-14). The second baseman can also receive the ball at the base and step backwards with the right foot, pushing off the bag towards the outfield with the left foot before making the throw on to first base (see pictures 5-15, 5-16). Finally, if the throw takes the player to the left field side of the base, they should follow the throw with the right foot and step towards the outfield before planting and throwing. Whichever method the second baseman

5-14: On a throw right to their chest, a second baseman can take their right foot across the bag towards third base before planting and throwing

5-15: The second basemen can also receive the ball at the bag before stepping backwards with their right foot (towards right field), pushing off the bag with their left foot and then planting and throwing

uses, they should get to the bag early and keep their feet moving so that they can be ready to receive a flip or throw and provide a good target for their teammate.

From the shortstop position, once the fielder gets to second base, he should set up with his right foot on the back corner of the bag and his shoulders square to the second baseman (see picture 5-17)—if the second baseman is fielding the ground ball. His left foot will step towards the thrown ball, leading him into his throwing motion. After receiving the throw, the shortstop should get his left shoulder pointed

5-16: The second basemen can also receive the ball at the bag before stepping backwards with their right foot (towards right field), pushing off the bag with their left foot and then planting and throwing

toward first base so that he can make a strong, accurate throw to first (see picture 5-18).

When receiving a double play feed from the first baseman who is playing in front of the first base bag (closer to home plate), the shortstop should set up with his left foot on the inside of the bag, facing the first baseman. After receiving the throw, he just has to get his front shoulder pointed towards first, push off his right leg, and throw back to first. If the first baseman is playing behind the runner (on the outfield side of the baseline between first and second), the shortstop will receive the throw the same way he would from a second baseman. It is critical that the shortstop sets up on the same side of the baseline as the first baseman. By doing so, the shortstop creates a clear throwing lane, and thus decreases the risk of hitting the runner with a throw or making a poor throw. In either case, instead of getting one or two outs on the play, an error is made, and they get no outs.

It is crucial for infielders to always use two hands whenever they're fielding a ground ball or receiving a throw from a teammate. What I mean by this is that the throwing hand should be right next to the glove

5-17: To turn a double play, a shortstop should set up with his right foot on the back corner of the bag and his shoulders square to his teammate

5-18: The shortstop will stride towards the thrown ball with his left foot before receiving and then getting his left shoulder pointed towards first base

hand, and as the ball contacts the glove, the throwing hand secures the ball, and transfers the ball into a throwing (or tagging) position. Not only does this facilitate quick transfers but it also is going to help them field the ball more cleanly resulting in fewer errors.

Something that happens a lot at the youth level is when a middle infielder fielding a double play ball is just a few feet from the bag but fires an overhand toss too hard to his teammate. On balls that force them to move towards second base or ones that are hit directly at them, middle infielders should use an underhand flip to get the ball to their teammate at second base. The three most important aspects of a good underhand flip are:

5-19: On an underhand flip, middle infielders should always stay low, flip firmly, and finish with the hand high

1. Staying low and using the lower half to generate momentum towards the target

2. Flipping the ball firmly and keeping the throwing hand behind the ball

3. Finishing with throwing hand high and following the ball after it is flipped (see pictures 5-19, 5-20 and 5-21)

Players should remember the 3 "T's": Transfer, Tuck and Toss. On all underhand flips, middle infielders should use their legs to generate the momentum towards second base. A good underhand flip should look

5-20: On an underhand flip, middle infielders should always stay low, flip firmly, and finish with the hand high

5-21: On an underhand flip, middle infielders should always stay low, flip firmly, and finish with the hand high

smooth and natural, not rushed. Regularly practicing underhand flips is essential to being able to perform them well in game situations.

And one final but important point on potential double play balls. Be sure to get one out—preferably the lead runner. Rushing and committing an error and getting no outs is always worse than getting one out!

Covering On Steal Attempts

Another important aspect of middle infield play is covering second base when the other team is attempting to steal. As this is considered a somewhat advanced game rule, many youth leagues either do not allow stealing, or the rule is modified as to when a runner may initially leave a base on an attempted steal. On steals of second base, as soon as he sees the runner in motion, the second baseman or shortstop should run to the bag in preparation for the catcher's throw. (As players get older and develop a better feel for the game, they may delay their "break" toward second base until they know the ball isn't hit toward them. This, however, takes a great deal of timing and understanding of many factors, including the speed of the runner, the throwing ability of the catcher, the game situation, etc.).

Generally, the shortstop will cover second base on a steal attempt when a left-handed hitter is at the plate while the second baseman will cover the bag when a righty is up at bat. In theory, this minimizes the chances that a ground ball or line drive will be hit towards the position vacated by the shortstop or second baseman. However, players (and coaches) should use their common sense. If there is a left-handed hitter at the plate who has been hitting ground balls to the shortstop all game, it would be wise for the second baseman to cover the bag on a steal.

It is critical that the second baseman and shortstop communicate with one another as to who will be covering the bag. This is typically done with an open mouth (indicating "you") or a closed mouth (indicating "me") signaled by one middle infielder to the other. This communication happens before each pitch, and the players hide this signal from the hitting team by holding their gloves up near the face so only their teammate can see the sign.

5-22: When covering on a steal attempt, middle infielders should set up by straddling the second base bag in order to receive the throw

A ball thrown by the catcher moves faster than a middle infielder can move their arm to tag a runner, so infielders should use this to their advantage by letting the ball travel

further in the first place. Therefore, middle infielders should
set up by straddling the second
base bag in order to receive
throws from the catcher (see
picture 5-22). However, if they
recognize the ball is thrown
off-line, they should try and
cut the ball off before it gets
through the infield, and perhaps leading to the runner
going to third. The player
should also be sure to cut the
ball off before reaching second
base when the runner is clearly
going to be safe. The defense
does not want or need to give
up extra bases for no reason.

5-23: Common Mistake: setting up in
front of the bag

Some coaches teach middle
infielders to set up in front of
second base on a steal attempt (see picture 5-23). This not only makes
it more difficult for players to reach back and tag the runner, but, more
importantly, it is generally slower. However, with catchers who don't
yet have strong enough throwing arms, you may have a better chance
to tag the runner out by being in front of rather than straddling the
base. This can also be a safer play for the infielder to receive the ball
and be more out of the way of the runner sliding into the base.

When a middle infielder puts the tag on a runner attempting to steal a
base, they should snap the glove straight down on the runner's foot (on
accurately thrown balls). If the glove stays on the bag with a runner
sliding in, he will risk having the ball knocked out of his glove. Furthermore, snapping the tag down and then back up helps to "sell" the tag
to the umpire (unlike MLB, youth baseball doesn't have replay review!).

Of course, the middle infielder may need to tag the runner somewhere other than on their foot if they are not executing a conventional feet first slide.

Rundowns

Something that is often overlooked during team practices is how to properly execute a rundown when a runner is hung up between two bases. It may only be an important a few times per season but if you don't practice it then don't expect to get an out when it happens in a game situation. Your team needs to practice rundowns with a live runner. An ideal rundown is one in which the defensive team gets the runner moving full speed in one direction (preferably back toward they base they came from) before making one throw in order to tag the runner out. While this may not always happen, it is a good goal to shoot for and encourages fielders to minimize the number of throws they make. After all, the more throws made during a rundown, the greater the chance that an error will be made and the runner will be safe.

5-24: In a rundown situation, the player with the ball should establish a throwing lane between himself and his teammate, and should get the ball out of his glove and into his throwing hand to chase the runner

In a rundown, the first thing the player holding the ball needs to do is establish a throwing lane. By this I mean he needs to get to the inside or outside of the runner's base path and ensure that the teammate receiving the throw is on the same side of the base path as the thrower (see picture 5-24). This helps minimize the chance that a throw will cut across the baseline and risk hitting the runner. Once the infielder gets the runner moving in one direction, he should get the ball out of his glove and into his throwing hand, holding it in a position where he can throw from. Infielders with the ball should run full speed at the runner, forcing him to run hard so that it is more difficult for him to change directions when a throw is made.

Infielders need to be ready to throw the ball at all times but should avoid pump faking. Why? While pump faking may serve to temporarily deceive the runner, it can also deceive teammates of the thrower as well and sometimes leads to inadvertent or errant throws when a ball slips out of the fielder's hand. A good team that knows how to execute a rundown should not need to use pump fakes.

The defensive player who is at the base where the runner is going should also be preparing for the throw. This player should have their glove up at about shoulder height to give their teammate a target. They should also be creeping toward the runner in order to "squeeze" them to end the rundown more quickly.

Keep in mind that mastering rundowns is difficult, even for skilled players at higher levels of the game. Coaches should at the very least allow for some practice time to work on rundowns just to give their players some experience, and when a rundown situation occurs in a game, your players will know what to do and won't be caught off guard.

Summary

Each one of the infield positions is quite unique, and experience is always the best teacher. Players who want to be close to the action, have good, quick instincts, and understand the flow of the game are usually good candidates for the infield. Coaches should be regularly reminding infielders where to position themselves, what the game situation is (number of outs, number of the batter in the order, etc.), and hitter tendencies (if they are known). With lots of practice repetitions to improve their individual skills, and lots of simulated game situation experiences, your infielders will develop the confidence necessary to help your team succeed.

Chapter 6

Outfielding

I t's the top of the 9th . . . two outs . . . runner on first, and the home team is ahead by a run. The pitcher delivers the ball to the batter. The ball is crushed off the bat . . . it's headed toward the fence in left-center. The center fielder sprints toward it . . . he leaps, stretches and snatches the baseball just before it sails over the fence. Out! Game Over!

In the game of baseball, one never knows which player will be in the position to make a play with the game on the line. One thing is for sure though – if you play enough games, you WILL get that opportunity! For those who play the outfield, it takes a great deal of practice, patience and discipline to master these all-important positions.

The outfielders are the three fielders referred to as the left fielder, center fielder and right fielder, and are the last line of defense on the baseball field (left, center and right are for a person standing at home plate looking out to the field). On a play-by-play basis, outfielders are generally less directly involved in the game than the other positions. An entire game can go by without a fly ball or ground ball being hit to a particular outfielder. For younger kids who may not have developed the ability to be able to focus for long periods of time, playing the outfield will challenge their patience. It is important for youth baseball coaches to remind young baseball players that outfielders DO have a responsibility on every play. Whether that is handling a ball hit to them, backing up other fielders, or communicating to teammates, the outfielder always needs to be prepared for action.

The outfield positions are often the most neglected in terms of instruction at a young age. Perhaps it is somewhat justifiable given how few balls make it to the outfield in typical games for young players. Thus, weaker fielders tend to be placed in the outfield in youth baseball and coaches focus more on instructing players who tend to have a larger impact on the game. This does an enormous disservice to young outfielders' development and, in turn, the team's success. (Fortunately, some leagues require all players to play some time in the outfield, which is great for developing players' knowledge of and ability to play various positions). Though his efforts may not jump out on the stat sheet, a knowledgeable, athletically capable outfielder is invaluable to a team.

Job Description

The primary job of an outfielder is to catch fly balls and field balls hit to them on the ground. Outfielders also have the challenging job of chasing down hard hit balls that get past them and go to the outfield fence or ricochet around the corners or other areas of the outfield. If not fielded properly, a ball hit to the outfield can quickly turn into an adventure. Conversely, with a ball in play in the outfield, a player with a strong and accurate arm will sometimes have the opportunity to throw out a base runner trying to take an extra base.

Speed and arm strength are both desirable traits for outfielders, but these tools should be developed in addition to fielding skills. These finer, more nuanced skills include: positioning, judging balls off the bat, judging the spin of a ball in the air, and playing balls correctly off of fences and walls. Some of these skills seem to be becoming lost arts. It amazes me every time I watch televised games how few outfielders I see who look comfortable fielding balls off the wall. Practicing playing balls off the wall for a few minutes every so often during practice is time well spent. Not everybody will have the arm strength of an Byron Buxton, Bryce Harper, Yasiel Puig, Mookie Betts or Aaron Judge, but any determined player can perfect proper techniques to maximize their natural talent. Having these skills may not get a player drafted by a major league team, but they will make players and their teams more successful. It is important to recognize that these skills can only be developed through practice and repetition.

Outfielders become more important to their teams when kids move up to the big (90' bases) diamond where outfielders have much more field space to cover, longer throws to make, and are involved in far more plays. Though some kids might feel slighted being asked to play the outfield, youth coaches should always strive to reinforce the responsibilities, importance and value of being a quality outfielder. Being able to play the outfield well is a great way for a player to get into the lineup because high school and college teams tend to lack players who are both skilled *and* enthusiastic about playing there. The ability to play multiple positions well always make a player more valuable to his team and gives him a better chance for playing time. If kids don't think that outfielders are that important or even part of the spotlight, there are plenty of examples to point to in major league baseball such as: Mike Trout, Lorenzo Cain, Jason Heyward, Aaron Judge, Yoenis Cespedes, Byron Buxton, Mookie Betts, Bryce Harper, Kevin Kiermaier, Bradley Zimmer, or a host of other outfield stars.

It's also important to remember that playing in the outfield tends to put less strain on the body than playing other positions does (unless a player is reckless and runs into outfield fences and walls often). Outfielders are typically afforded the opportunity to make fewer throws per game than infielders and catchers and as a result, can "save" their arms if they need to. However, at the highest levels, one common theme is that there will always be a number of outfielders who are among the most productive *offensive* players in their league. In order to become a complete outfielder, young ballplayers should strive to be impactful with their bat as well.

⊘ ⊘ ⊘ ⊘ ⊘ ⊘ ⊘ **Story from Dan** ⊘ ⊘ ⊘ ⊘ ⊘ ⊘ ⊘

Thinking back to my minor league playing time, I'll never forget my first year in Great Falls as a catcher. We started the season 20-16 and then won 30 out of the next 34 games. We had Pedro Martinez and the right fielder was Raul Mondesi. We were playing Salt Lake City in Great Falls. In the top of the 9th, up one run, our closer (Gordon Tipton) was in the game. There was one out with man on a second base, and there's a base hit to Mondesi, who threw me a laser on a line, when I dropped down to make the tag, the runner was only half way home so we got him in a rundown, and tagged him out, so the batter gets to second during the rundown. The next batter gets a base hit to Mondesi again, who starts laughing, because he knows they have to send him with two outs in the bottom of the ninth, and he had one of the best arms I've ever seen, and this next base runner is out by 20 feet!

Positioning

Many young players (and inexperienced coaches as well) believe that each player in the field has a "set" position. This is where every defensive player positions themselves in the same spot for every batter in the lineup. However, if you watch closely, you'll notice that during ballgames, major leaguers often make subtle changes in where they are positioned based on the hitter, field conditions, and the game situation. (In recent years, shifting an extra player to one side of the infield against pull hitters has become more commonplace.) It is crucial for coaches to shift defensive players according to where the player is more likely to hit the ball.

For most batters, outfielders will use "straightaway" positioning. This is the default from which all shifts are made. For the left fielder, it is on a straight line extending from first base to second base into the outfield. For right fielders, it's on the line from third and second base into the outfield, and for center it's in a straight line extending from the plate, the pitcher's mound, and second base. Center fielders will generally have to move two or three steps to their right (for right handed batters) or left (for left handed batters) from that straight on position, or his view of the batter will be obscured by the pitcher.

For the youngest players, the straightaway position is just fine in order for the player to get a "feel" for their position. However, as players move up the ranks, they will need to learn how and why they should make certain shifts during a game by listening to and speaking with their coaches. Why should outfielders make these shifts? It's a calculated risk, actually. One never knows of course exactly where a batter will hit the ball in a particular at bat, but through experience, players can increase their odds of getting an out by moving to where they think the batter is likely to hit the ball based upon the batter's history and the type of pitcher on the mound.

From the straightaway position, outfielders should shift from batter to batter (and at the highest levels pitch to pitch) after considering the following items: hitter tendencies ("pull" hitter or "spray" hitter, power hitter or "singles" hitter, etc.), pitcher considerations (how hard he throws, location of pitches, etc.), weather factors (wind, sun, etc.), game situation (score, inning, runners on base, count, etc.), field conditions (wet or dry, high grass or low grass, etc.), personal abilities (arm strength, speed, etc.), and the abilities of one's teammates. If a coach does not shift the outfielders during the game, it is generally the center fielder's responsibility to position himself and the corner outfielders according to the factors above.

Set-Up (Ready Position)

An outfielder should get into his ready position as the pitcher delivers the ball to the plate so that he can quickly react to a ball hit in any direction. There are numerous ways that this is taught, but the two most common are *squared up* and *angled off*. In order to *square up*, the player will directly face the hitter, keeping his legs a little wider than shoulder-width apart, bending his knees slightly, and squatting slightly. The hands should be off the knees (free) in front of the player, and he should be in a pretty standard "athletic stance." By setting up in this fashion, the lower half of the body becomes engaged as the pitch approaches the batter. This is the most common method.

Some coaches teach their outfielders to *angle off* their bodies by dropping either foot back such that they will be at a 45° angle to the batter (see picture 6-1). There are pros and cons to this approach. Angling off the body is largely absent from higher levels of baseball because it prevents players from pursuing balls as effectively that are hit to the opposite side that they are angled. However, it also serves as a reminder for outfielders to take their first step back when a fly ball is hit their way—a cue that younger players sometimes need. As a rule of thumb for any outfielder when reading the flight of a ball, if unsure,

6-1: An example of an angled off set up for outfielders

the first step should always be back. This is because it is far easier and quicker to come in on a ball than go back if the initial assessment of a fly ball was incorrect.

Outfielders will learn to "read" balls off the bat more accurately with practice. The best time to get repetitions with balls hit to the outfield is during batting practice, as the ball will come off the bat in a game-like way. During batting practice, players should not waste their time in the field loafing around and socializing until it's their turn to hit! They should use this time to improve their defensive game.

Catching fly balls

Catching fly balls is an out-fielder's single greatest responsibility. Ideally, the ball will be caught with the fielder directly under the ball as it descends. Outfielders should always try to quickly get to the spot where the ball would land. This is because it is much easier to track a moving ball while the body is stationary. Tracking a ball while on the run creates somewhat of a bouncing effect. *Drifting* (moving slowly toward the ball and "meeting it" as it falls) is a common mistake out-fielders make, and is sometimes a result of laziness. It might feel smoother and seem cooler than sprinting to a ball and settling under it, but drifting towards a fly ball is far riskier.

6-2: Outfielders should position the fingers of their glove hand so that they are pointing towards the sky, with both hands positioned above the eyes

When the outfielder is in a position where he can catch the ball, the fingers in his glove-hand should point upward toward the sky, and both hands should be positioned above the eyes (see picture 6-2). Ideally, he will have plenty of time to track it and catch it with two hands. This is the safest way to catch a fly ball. It is important to note here that a player does not *actually* use both hands in the catching sequence. The throwing hand should move toward the glove as the ball is caught. This creates balance for the player, allows for a quick transfer if the player needs to throw quickly, and will allow for a quick recovery if the ball is bobbled. Rhythm and momentum should be maintained

6-3: A proper drop step to chase a ball over the outfielder's right shoulder

6-4: A proper drop step to chase a ball over the outfielder's left shoulder

throughout the process. It should look and feel smooth when done properly.

⦿ ⦿ ⦿ ⦿ ⦿ ⦿ ⦿ ⦿ **Story from Dan** ⦿ ⦿ ⦿ ⦿ ⦿ ⦿ ⦿
Drill—The Drop Step Drill

All you need is some open space and a few baseballs for this drill. One at a time, players should take their ready position a few feet in front of the coach, whom they are facing, and on a signal, perform a drop step and chase a ball thrown over their head to either the right or left. Coaches can point right or left to direct players to go in that direction or simply have them react to the ball.

Make sure that players' first step is a correctly executed drop step on an angle that will give them a good route to the ball. If players need a challenge, try throwing balls directly over their head, as that is the toughest angle an outfielder will have to take.

On fly balls that are hit over an outfielders' head, again, their first step needs to be a *drop step*. This is when a player simply takes a diagonal step backwards with one foot to the side that the ball is hit, opening up their body in such a way that it allows them to direct a running pathway to the ball (see pictures 6-3 and 6-4). The exact angle of the step depends on how the outfielder judges the ball. If the ball is directly over the outfielder's head, the angle of their step should be 180° to home plate.

For catching balls on the run, outfielders should practice catching balls with just their glove hand (the throwing hand is in natural running/ balance position). An outfielder's range of motion is limited by using two hands and could prevent them from making a play, especially on balls they have to stretch for. One thing that younger players struggle with is when to put up their glove. Running with the glove up and arm extended is slower than running with it naturally by the hip. Outfielders should remember that raising the glove takes very little time. The glove really isn't needed until the ball approaches the hand. The extra couple of feet that can be gained from running with the glove down could mean the difference between an out and a hit for the opposing team.

The only exception to this is on a ball hit in the air and the fielder is looking toward the sun. Outfielders need repetitions and correct technique. Sunglasses can help, but getting the glove up early is key. When the fielder's eyes are behind the glove, he is less likely to be blinded by the sun and can see the ball for as long as possible before he ultimately loses it briefly in the sun (see picture 6-5). The longer he can see the ball, the better read he will have on where the ball will likely end up, giving him a better chance to make the catch. If an outfielder does lose sight of the ball and knows he will not make a play, he should wave both arms above his head to communicate to other fielders that he has lost it. There is no reason to wait to do this if he has, in fact, lost the ball in the sun. The sooner he communicates this, the better the chance that he will give his teammates sufficient time to make the play or at the very least, limit the number of bases runners advance.

6-5: Outfielders should use their gloves to shield their eyes from the sun on high fly balls

Communication

There are some universally accepted ways a player can call for a ball. The two main ones are saying "ME" or "YOU," and calling BALL. If both fielders call out BALL, there's no way for one of them to tell the other that he should take it, thus ME/YOU is more commonly used. With ME/YOU, there is a give and take as well as a way to distinguish between fielders.

In terms of priority, the center fielder is the captain of the outfield and if he calls for the ball, the corner outfielders should generally defer to him. If any outfielder calls for a ball, infielders should generally defer as well because again, it is easier for the player moving forward to catch the ball. Regardless of what position a player occupies, any communication should be decisive, loud, and repeated multiple times. If a player says ME just once, quietly (or even worse, not at all), it could lead to the play not being made, and perhaps a dangerous collision. At younger levels, when balls fall in between two or three players that could've made the play, it is almost always due to a communication error.

Fielding Balls on the Ground

On ground balls hit toward them, there are generally two ways outfielders can choose to field the ball: stationary and on the move. In

6-6: In situations where there is no chance to throw out a runner, an outfielder may drop to a knee to field the ball

Caption: 6-7: When fielding a ground ball in the outfield, outfielders may choose to field the ball off their glove side leg

situations where there is no chance to throw out a runner, a player may decide to drop to a knee to field the ball (see picture 6-6). This method is substantially slower, but significantly reduces the chance the ball will get past them (and in turn prevents runners from taking extra bases). To do this, outfielders should center the ball to their body and drop one knee to the ground when the ball is 10-15 away from them, and place the glove out in front to receive the ball. Once the ball is secured, the fielder hops up quickly and throws the ball into the infield.

One other situation where outfielders may choose this option is when the field conditions are less than ideal, such as choppy or wet grass. When warming up the fielders will know if balls will take "true" bounces, or if the bounces are unpredictable. When field conditions are bad, the player must decide if it's a "do or die" situation and play the ball accordingly.

With runners on base, outfielders should move through ground balls in a direct line without stopping and let their momentum take them towards their target. They should be aggressive but under control, using choppy steps as they get close to the ball to maintain balance and body control. The ball should be fielded out in front and then the outfielder needs to take a crow hop if a quick throw is necessary (see picture 6-7).

Throwing

An outfielder's objective when throwing a ball that he has fielded is to get the ball back into the infield (*where* it needs to go), as quickly and accurately as possible. Having a strong throwing arm definitely helps, but utilizing proper footwork and taking optimal angles to balls can make up for a weaker throwing arm.

On plays where runners are tagging up trying to advance, outfielders should try to get "behind" the ball to gain momentum through the catch in order to make a stronger throw. Obviously the first objective is to catch the ball. Outfielders should never let balls drop when they could possibly be caught. However, if time allows, the outfielder should try to get to a spot about 5-10 feet behind where the ball will land. The spot should also be in a direct line with the base to which they are throwing. Sometimes this means taking a path to a ball that isn't a straight line, but ultimately this will save time on the throw. The distance between the player and where the catch is made should be covered gradually. Rather than an all-out sprint, the outfielder should start slowly but pick up momentum such that they are moving much faster through the ball as it is caught. This is obviously an advanced skill and should only be attempted by outfielders who have mastered consistently catching routine fly balls.

There are two different approaches to playing a ground ball that needs to be thrown as quickly as possible. One is fielding off the glove side leg, and the other is fielding the ball on throwing side leg. The most commonly taught method involves fielding the ball off the glove-side leg (see picture 6-7 in the previous section). Here, the fielder can push off that leg as they pick up the ball, plant their throwing side leg, take a quick hop on the same leg and finally plant the glove-side leg again as they make the throw. For a righty it should go left-right-left. If an outfielder fields a ball off their throwing side leg, they should plant that leg, pick up the ball, and quickly hop on the same leg as they return to an upright position, land with the same leg, then plant their glove-side leg and throw (right-right-left for righties). Fielding off either foot isn't more correct than the other and the particular crow-hops aren't exclusive to each foot. It is a simply a style that players will develop.

Transfer and Hitting the Cut-Off

When fielding balls off the ground, outfielders should try to transfer the ball from the glove to the throwing hand out and down in front of the body. The quicker the ball gets into the throwing hand, the quicker they can throw it into the infield. Outfielders should "find" the four-seam grip during the transfer and throw "over the top" (not side-arm) as best they can. This will help the ball carry with backspin, and go straighter. It will also allow for a truer skip if it bounces.

Outfielders should attempt to throw "through the cut-off man's head" and follow through aggressively. Lobbing a ball in and missing a cut-off man are both ineffective, in addition to looking bad to fans, coaches, and players alike.

An outfielder's goal should not be to throw out runners, but rather to make strong, accurate throws consistently to their correct teammate. When the opportunity presents itself to "air one out," then they can do so, but only if it's a "do or die" situation. Most throws should be balls that can be potentially cut off so that other base runners cannot advance. Again, remind younger players to throw *through* cut-off men if possible. An ideal throw should be low enough that it can be cut-off if necessary, but it should also have enough velocity that it can reach the desired base (in the air or on a bounce or two) if the infielder lets it go.

The best time to get reps with this is during practice or during infield/outfield warm-ups before a game. Players should put full effort into their throws and focus on the fundamentals. They should be reminded that by taking these repetitions at full speed during practice, they are preparing themselves to make these plays at "game" speed during games.

Some players who played in prior generations believe that the ability to make strong, accurate throws from the outfield has become deemphasized in today's generation of ballplayers. Former Detroit Tiger outfielder and Hall of Famer Al Kaline has said:

"The outfielders really need to be practicing making long throws because sometimes you can go several games before you have to make a long or hard throw. They don't do it at all. Today the outfielders play long catch before the game, and they work on the outfield walls when they go to another ballpark but they don't regularly practice throwing home like we did when I played. They just don't do it. Throwing in game conditions is a lot different then just playing long catch in the outfield. In a game you have to move your feet a lot faster and you don't have time to set up and throw. Today it seems when they have to do it they are not very accurate with their throws. I don't know why they don't practice throwing home at least once every series just to get as used to game situations as you possibly can. I don't think anybody does it anymore."

Whether this sentiment is true or not, it is important for outfielders to work on their throws to all of the bases, as one never knows when one single throw to a base may affect the outcome of a game.

Backing up plays

Backing up plays is the least exciting job for an outfielder and a responsibility that most often gets neglected at the youth level. No player should be stationary on *any* ball in play, outfielders included! For example, imagine a routine ground ball to the shortstop with no runners on base: the shortstop obviously fields it, the second baseman covers second, the third basemen has third, the catcher and right fielder back up first base, the pitcher moves towards first base, and the left and centerfielder back up short. Notice that every player has a place to be on the field, regardless of where the ball is hit. Outfielders' backups usually involve backing up infielders since the majority of plays in a game take place in the infield.

On balls hit to the outfield, the adjacent outfielder (or outfielders) to the player making the play should back him up. It is important to remember that when called off of a ball in play, the other outfielder(s) should not give up on the play, but should back up their teammate in case of an error or unexpected bounce. Especially for younger players, coaches should provide positive reinforcement and praise for backing up plays. It is a preventative measure because although it likely will not have an impact on the game's outcome, when an error does occur, the back up needs to be there. One never knows when an innocent back up play can turn an outfielder into the player who saved the game!

Chapter 7

Catching

The runner is barreling around third base at full speed, heading for home as the tying run in the last inning. The center fielder charges the baseball, scoops it up, and launches a throw toward the plate. The catcher receives the one hop throw and twists toward the runner who is sliding into home. The catcher tags the runner just before he reaches the plate . . . and when the dust settles the runner is called OUT! Game Over!

Aside from the pitcher, the catcher is the most important player on the field. He is directly involved on every single pitch (although he usually does not touch the baseball when the batter hits it). Being a catcher is great for kids who feel the desire to be constantly involved, and who may get bored with the lack of action at other positions on the field.

The catcher is also unique in his positioning—he's the only player who sets up in foul territory facing the rest of the fielders—giving him a clear view of the entire field and all of his teammates. For this reason, it's critical that the catcher be a true team leader on the field of play. Catchers need to be confident and vocal to give direction to their teammates for proper positioning before the pitch and during specific plays once the ball is in play.

Catchers need to be extremely tough as well. The position is physically demanding. Constant squatting and standing places a lot of stress on the lower body, and the volume of throws catchers are required to make can tax their throwing arm and shoulder. Catchers *must* take care of their arms, as they make just as many throws (if not more) than any other player on the field. Warming up properly, having sound throwing mechanics, and stretching are essential for catchers on a daily basis.

Catchers should take pride in the fact that they play a less glamorous but critically important position. Particularly at the younger age levels, a good catcher will save his team lots of runs over the course of a season just by keeping pitched balls in front of him and runners from advancing on the bases. Catchers will get nicked up by tipped foul balls and pitched balls in the dirt. Hot days can be even hotter with all the gear catchers must wear. Just like linemen of a football team, catchers don't always get credit where it is due, but their role on the team is essential. They don't often make the video highlights on sports' news segments for blocking a ball or directing a play to the right base at the right time, but these plays can have an enormous influence on the outcome of a game.

⊘ ⊘ ⊘ ⊘ ⊘ ⊘ ⊘ **Story from Dan** ⊘ ⊘ ⊘ ⊘ ⊘ ⊘ ⊘

I didn't catch until senior year of high school. I was a middle infielder. I was being told that if I wanted to play in college, it would be better to convert to be a catcher. At that time, there weren't as many people wanting to catch and there were lots of middle infielders. After I got drafted, I became really good defensively with the L.A. Dodgers organization—they had a "string area" for pitchers to get them to throw to specific parts of the strike zone. I caught pitchers for about four hours per day in the bullpen. Catching so many pitchers with different pitches and approaches for so many hours, helped make me a really good defensive catcher who knew how to work with different pitchers.

Stance

Everything a catcher does should be athletic and comfortable. The more natural the movements are, the more confident and repeatable the actions will be. Depending on the game situation, catchers will adjust their set-up position (stance) accordingly.

Note: Younger players who play with modified rules (no stealing, no advancing on balls that get behind the catcher, etc.) should focus on basic set-up and receiving skills. Advanced players who play with regular rules will need to understand the variations in setting-up and receiving.

7-1: With no runners on base and less than two strikes, catchers should set up in a Primary Stance

With no runners on base and less than 2 strikes, a catcher should be in a *primary stance*. The catcher should center their body 1-2 feet directly behind home plate with their feet pointed outwards and slightly wider than shoulder-width apart (like a defensive stance in basketball, only in a squatting position). They should be leaning somewhat forward with their body weight centered on the balls and inside of the feet. The back should be slightly flexed forward so that their upper body is not in a rigid, upright position. The glove arm should be held just above the knee (not resting on it) with a relaxed, loose wrist. The arm should be partially extended (not fully extended, or too close to the body) in a comfortable position. The glove should be turned slightly clockwise to best receive pitches. The throwing hand should be kept behind the back just above the throwing side heel to protect it from foul tips (see picture 7-1).

With runners on base, or with two strikes on the batter, a catcher should set-up in a *secondary stance*. The right foot should be slightly

7-2: With runners on base or with two strikes on the batter, catchers should adopt a Secondary Stance in which they are a bit raised up higher in the air

7-3: Catchers should give signs with the throwing hand in the cup area in order to hide them from the opposing team

staggered so that the front of the foot is in line with the middle of the left foot (or instep). The catcher should also raise his buttocks just a few inches higher in the air. The catcher should remain low (as a result his back should now be flatter and closer to parallel with the ground), but he needs to be ready to move his feet while keeping his target low for the pitcher (see picture 7-2). Now the off-hand could be kept balled in a loose fist *behind* the glove, though it is perfectly fine (and likely safer) to still keep it behind the body above the right heel. Either location is fine as long as the off-hand is being protected behind something and is not susceptible to foul tips.

Giving Signs

At more advanced levels where the catcher is delivering signs to the pitcher, the sign is given just before the catcher sets in their primary or secondary stance. Signs should be given with the throwing hand in the "cup" area with the glove arm resting below the left knee—which keeps the opposing team from seeing the signs (see picture 7-3). When the pitcher has received the signs, the catcher gets into ready position.

⊘ ⊘ ⊘ ⊘ ⊘ ⊘ ⊘ Story from Dan ⊘ ⊘ ⊘ ⊘ ⊘ ⊘ ⊘
Left-Handed Catchers

Watch a college or professional baseball game and you will rarely if ever see a left-handed catcher. Since 1900, only 9 left-handed catchers have played in the Major Leagues! The only level where left-handed catchers are seen these days is at the youth level. There are a number of theories out there for why this is the case. A majority of batters are right-handed, so throws down to second are far more difficult for left-handed throwers. Additionally, it is harder for left-handed throwers to field bunts down the third base line and then angle their body to throw to first. Finally, plays at the plate would all have to be backhanded to tag the runner, which is much slower and arguably more dangerous. These reasons make good sense at higher levels, however at youth levels they are not necessarily that important.

For a youth team, if the best catcher—a kid with a good arm who can receive and block well—happens to be left-handed, then it would be fine to put him back there part of the time. I would rather have a player catching who can keep the ball in front of him who happens to throw with the "wrong" hand rather than a right-handed thrower who has no idea what he is doing. Though they might not have a long-term future behind the plate due to conventional wisdom, let your left-handers try it if you think they can handle it. And be sure they learn to play other positions as well!

Receiving

As the bulk of the plays in a game will end up with the ball in the catcher's mitt, receiving is the most important part of a catcher's game. When receiving the ball, the catcher wants to help get his pitcher as many strikes as he can. The catcher should try to center everything, receiving the pitch with his body behind the baseball. As the pitcher is

7-4: When receiving the ball, the catcher should try to center everything by receiving the pitch with his body behind the baseball

winding up, the catcher should relax his wrist so that he is ready to receive. If the ball is slightly to the right or left of his set-up position, he should try to move behind it smoothly—not with sudden, herky-jerky motions (see picture 7-4).

When receiving the ball, the catcher wants to make pitches look as good as possible to the umpire. This *does not* mean moving the ball back over the plate once he has caught it, but rather "framing" pitches in such a way that they appear as strikes to the umpire. If a pitch is clearly a ball, trying to frame it will only hurt a catcher's standing with the umpire so players should not waste their time. The same goes for pitches that are clearly strikes—in this case framing is not necessary (see pictures 7-5 through 7-8). Contrary to what many players may think, umpires *do* have a strong grasp of the strike zone and it's likely to your advantage not to insult umpires by holding pitches for a long time that are obvious one way or the other. It is important to only hold pitches that appear close to being strikes. Pitches that are "on the black" or the corners of the plate are the ones the catcher wants to frame. He should stiffen his wrist once he has received the ball and hold it there just a split second longer for the umpire to think about to possibly get that crucial strike call.

7-5: Receiving a pitch away (to a right-handed hitter)

7-6: Receiving a pitch in (to a right-handed hitter)

A good receiver of the ball will give confidence to his pitcher and help him to get into a better rhythm. Above everything a catcher does, his number one priority is to keep the pitcher focused as he is *the* most important player on the field. The more a catcher knows about his pitcher (mechanics, tendencies, pitch selection, emotions, etc.) the better. If a catcher can identify problems their pitcher may be having during a game, then he can help correct them with a quick mound visit (after calling for time). He can also help by giving different targets. For example, if a pitcher is consistently missing high in the strike zone, the catcher could set-up with a lower than normal target. Even if it is just encouraging the pitcher or being positive and upbeat, if a catcher can make the pitcher feel comfortable, he is doing his job effectively.

7-7: Receiving a pitch up in the strike zone

7-8: Receiving a pitch down in the strike zone

When a catcher may need to throw to a base, he wants to receive the ball as deep (close to his body) as possible. If he reaches out for a pitch or extends his arm completely so that his glove is closer to the batter, not only is he more likely to be called for catcher's interference by touching the hitter's bat on a swing, but he is also wasting time. The ball moves much faster than the glove can with the ball in it. Players must remember that if they are reaching out for the ball, they must bring the ball back to their body to prepare for a throw. Furthermore, "locking" (straightening) out the arm will make it hard for the catcher to adjust to late movement on a pitched ball. Simply put, catchers should allow the ball to travel into the glove rather than reaching out for it.

Ball Transfer and Throwing

When throwing, the first thing that must be done is the transfer of the ball from the glove to the throwing hand. The catcher can't throw until he gets the ball to his throwing hand. Immediately after catching the ball, he should bring his glove to the center of his body (in front of the chest) to meet the throwing hand. The glove hand releases pressure on the ball so that the throwing hand can quickly and easily remove the ball from the glove. Once the transfer is complete, he should bring the ball just behind his right ear to prepare for the throw. Simultaneously, the glove hand remains high with the front shoulder and elbow pointed

7-9: Transferring to a strong power position to throw the baseball

toward the target in what is known as the *power position* (see picture 7-9). One other thing to note here is that the catcher's throwing hand should "find" the four-seam grip during the transfer in order to make an accurate throw.

A second method that is commonly taught is to bring *both* the glove and throwing hand behind the ear and then transfer. I believe that this method is less desirable as it allows the ball to potentially move around in the glove, therefore making a quick transfer and proper four-seam grip more difficult.

When throwing to any base, the catcher should create momentum towards the target. If he is throwing to second base, upon receiving the ball his right foot should step forward a few inches so that it is parallel to the front of plate. He should then step with the left foot right behind the back tip of home plate. Catchers should try to avoid stepping on home plate because they could slip (and possibly injure themselves) and make a poor throw. As the front foot lands the front shoulder should be pointed towards second base. A strong follow through must occur as well so that the ball doesn't tail (spin and move from left to right). Everything should flow in a straight line towards second base. The marks on the dirt around home plate will show whether this has happened or not. Throughout the sequence, the catcher should stay low and athletic (fully using his lower half) so that he can throw the ball as hard and as quickly as he can.

While quickness is essential and develops more at higher levels, younger catchers should focus on taking their time with their throws rather than rushing. This leads to good form and mechanics. The most important thing is that the throw is accurate. A lot more base runners will be thrown out if the catcher can put the ball in a place where it is easy for the fielder to catch it and put the tag down. Coaches should remind kids that it is better to make a low throw rather than a high (and sometimes looping) throw. Too high a throw—though possibly impressive in showing the catcher's arm strength—gives the fielder no chance to make a play and potentially allows runners to take an extra base. Many young catchers may not even be able to reach second base with a throw in the air. A ball that is thrown low or that bounces will at least still give the fielder a chance to catch the ball and tag the runner out, or at least block the ball keeping it from going into the outfield.

When throwing to third, the mechanics remain the same, only everything moves in the direction of third base. On a steal attempt of third, if a righty is hitting, the catcher should step behind the batter when making the throw, creating an angle so that he has a clear lane to throw to third (see pictures 7-10, 7-11 and 7-12). If a lefty is up, the catcher

7-10: When throwing to third, catchers should step behind a right-handed hitter to create a clear throwing lane

7-11: When throwing to third, catchers should step behind a right-handed hitter to create a clear throwing lane

has no obstacles to worry about, so he can step straight toward third base. Again, the front shoulder should still point toward the base, there should be a complete follow through, and the catchers should stay low throughout. Quickness should be emphasized here because the throw to third is shorter than to second, so arm strength matters less.

7-12: When throwing to third, catchers should step behind a right-handed hitter to create a clear throwing lane

Blocking

Blocking pitches that bounce in the dirt is probably the aspect of the catcher position that is hardest for young catchers to learn. Many youngsters try to reach down and backhand balls or pick them cleanly from the dirt. This is far riskier and often leads to wild pitches and passed balls. However, with lots of practice, blocking balls becomes second nature.

A catcher should block the ball with his chest protector, not the glove. Not only is the chest protector far bigger, using it also ensures that the body is behind the ball as opposed to only using the glove, which is comparatively small.

The first action with blocking should be moving the glove down to the ground (hand open with the fingers in the glove pointed downward) and the throwing hand behind it. If the ball is to the left or right the glove should go first, and the body should follow ("leading with the glove"). Next, the catcher should quickly drop to his knees with his chest angled about 45 degrees towards the ground. The chin should

7-13: Proper blocking position with the chin tucked, chest angled, and the throwing hand behind the glove

7-14: When blocking balls, the catcher should beat the ball to the spot and angle his body to direct the ball toward the home plate area

be tucked to the chest—not facing away—as this is safer (the throat is protected) and creates a better angle to keep the ball in front (see picture 7-13). If the ball is to the right or left, the catcher should angle his body so that balls bouncing off him will fall back towards the home plate area. The goal here is for the catcher to beat the ball to the spot so that it does not get by him (see picture 7-14). When the ball gets there, the catcher should simply allow it to bounce off his chest protector so that he softens it and controls it.

One major challenge coaches encounter when teaching young catchers how to block is overcoming their fear of the ball. A lot of kids are afraid that absorbing the blow of the bounced pitch with their body will hurt and so they turn their head to the side when the ball bounces in. If this is the case, coaches can bounce balls from a shorter distance away or use tennis balls in drills until the player gets more comfortable with blocking and trusting that the equipment (and sound technique) will keep them safe (be sure that your players have good quality chest protectors, shin guards, masks, etc.). Confidence is built through repetition. Kids need to see a lot of pitches in order to learn what bouncing balls look like coming toward them. Once they can anticipate this, blocking will become easier. Catchers that consistently block balls effectively find it a great source of pride, not to mention it may help their team win the game.

Fielding Bunts (and slow rollers)

If a batter turns to attempt a bunt, the catcher must recognize this yet remain patient. He should anticipate being ready to move to the bunted ball, yet he cannot step out of his crouch in case the batter pulls the bat back or misses the ball. Once the ball is bunted, the catcher must quickly determine if he is in the best position to field it. Communication

7-15: When fielding bunts and slow rollers, catchers should stay low and point non-throwing shoulder towards base he is throwing to

is a must. If he is closest to the ball, he should yell "Me!" while getting to the ball as quickly as possible.

If the pitcher or first/third baseman is closer, the catcher still has a job to do. He should yell "You!" and then look up to see where the runners are and yell what base he should throw to or "Hold!" when they get to the ball. Again, the catcher is the only one who can see everything going on, so he needs to be decisive and loud on his calls.

7-16: When fielding bunts and slow rollers, catchers should stay low and point non-throwing shoulder towards base he is throwing to

When moving to a ball bunted on the ground, the catcher should stay low and get his

7-17: When fielding bunts and slow rollers, catchers should stay low and point non-throwing shoulder towards base he is throwing to

chest and body over the ball. Bending at the knees, the catcher should next bring his glove and bare hand together to pick up the ball at the same time. While doing this, he is simultaneously staying low and rotating his body to point his non-throwing shoulder at the base he is throwing to (see pictures 7-15, 7-16 and 7-17). He then throws, releases, and follows through. A catcher should not stop moving while picking up the ball but should keep his feet moving to get momentum towards his target. If the ball is bunted just inside the first base line, the catcher may need to field the ball first, and take a step in toward the mound in order to create a throwing lane so he doesn't have to throw over the runner.

Pop-Ups

On balls that are popped up near home plate, the catcher should step out in front of home plate, turn his body so his back is to the field of play, and remove and hold onto his mask as he locates the ball. Once he has located the ball, he should then toss his mask aside far enough away so that he won't trip over it (see pictures 7-18 and 7-19).

Catchers must understand that balls hit nearly straight up in the air have a great deal of backspin which makes the ball curve toward the field of play

7-18: On pop-ups in fair territory, catchers should try to turn and face home plate

as it descends. (The higher the ball is hit, the more spin it has, and the more it will curve toward the infield). The catcher should position

7-19: On pop-ups near home plate, catchers should remove their mask and toss it aside so that they don't trip over it

himself slightly behind where the ball looks like it will land in order to account for the motion of the ball. It is often necessary for catchers to continually adjust their position as the ball descends. Finally, he should see the ball all the way into his mitt and squeeze it with two hands (see pictures 7-20 and 7-21).

7-20: Keep moving towards the pop-up and see the ball into the mitt

7-21: Keep moving towards the pop-up and see the ball into the mitt and squeeze with both hands

Once he has secured the ball, he should turn back towards the field ready to make a throw if necessary. Again, the best way catchers can learn how to field pop-ups is with lots of repetition and practice!

Other Responsibilities

Catchers have other responsibilities as well. At some levels coaches count on them to call pitches (and the location of pitches as well). Catchers also must line up fielders on relay throws from the outfield. They should be alert to try and pick off runners when they have leads that are too big. Catchers must know how to receive pitch-outs. (These topics and more will be covered in our book outlining advanced skills & strategies.)

✪ ✪ ✪ ✪ ✪ ✪ ✪ *Story from Dan* ✪ ✪ ✪ ✪ ✪ ✪ ✪

My catching coach was Johnny Roseboro—and practicing for him was at times a grind—they were long and demanding but we got a lot out of it. There were all sorts of drills, known as the Catcher's Olympics, that we had to do for points. There were blocking drills where you had to keep the ball nearby for points. We made throws to second base and were awarded points for accuracy. We caught high pop-ups from a pitching machine pointed skyward. This machine was also used for receiving and blocking drills. We also worked on cut offs and relays, fielding bunts and throws to bases. We did have lots of fun, but everything was based upon the drills. Competing for points in his Olympics helped to keep our attention for a longer period of time.

Chapter 8

Base Running

I t's a tie game in the bottom of the last inning, with a runner on second base and two outs. The batter lines a base hit up the middle—the base runner rounds third and heads for home. The center fielder charges, fields the ball, and launches a throw toward the plate. The catcher receives the ball, puts down a tag just as the runner slides . . .

During the course of a multi-hour baseball game, there are a handful of plays when the crowd moves to the edge of their seats during a play. The drama plays out both in the field and on the base paths, and when the two intersect, there is a moment of truth—safe or out?

Baserunning is an often-overlooked facet of the game with many subtle nuances. Just as the defense wants to prevent the offense from taking extra bases and scoring runs, the offense wants to move runners along and take as many extra bases and score as many runs as they can. Baserunning is influenced both by mental preparation and instinct. Especially when players move up to higher levels of play, when on the bases, it's vital that the runner always knows the score, the number of outs, the count, the positioning and arm strength of the different fielders (and their tendencies) and be looking and listening for the base coaches' instructions.

Baserunning is just like every other aspect of baseball: skills are developed through practice. The more situations a player finds themselves in on the bases, the quicker and smarter they will be for future times they are in a similar situation.

A common misconception among younger players is that being fast equates to being a good base runner. Although it can make things easier if a player is naturally speedy, the reality is that anyone can become a much *better* base runner if they put the time and effort in and master the best techniques.

Proper running form can improve any player's speed. Runners should remember to keep their bodies relaxed with their heads and eyes up. They should also pump their arms straight forward and back—not across the body—reaching with their hands from back pocket to chin. Keeping these basic mechanics in mind, here is a tour around the bases.

Home to First

A base runner's responsibility starts even before stepping up to the plate because they have responsibilities while waiting on-deck. If a teammate is running to home on a play, the on-deck hitter should communicate with and signal to the runner whether or not to slide or remain standing up. (Note: In many youth baseball programs, if there is a play at the plate or other base, runners may be required to slide and/or avoid collisions.) Also, the on-deck hitter can let the batter know if a third strike has gotten away from the catcher, giving the hitter a chance to run to first base.

After swinging and contacting the ball, or on a dropped third strike, the batter becomes a base runner. On any ground ball to the infield or a hit to short right field, runners should *always* sprint 100% through first base. The same goes for routine pop-ups and fly balls - balls that *should* be caught by the defense sometimes are missed or dropped . . . even in the major leagues! Even the best players (including MLB players) make mistakes or can be tripped up by problematic weather conditions like wind, sun in their eyes, cloudy skies, poor visibility, etc.

On ground balls hit to the infield, the runner should run straight toward first base right out of the batter's box. About halfway down

8-1: Baserunners should hit the front part of the first base bag with either foot

8-2: Baserunners should break down along the baseline after hitting the base

the line, the runner should visually pick up first base. It doesn't matter which foot the runner hits the base with, but they should try to hit the front part of the base. After running hard *through* the base, the runner should "break down" (slow down) by stuttering their feet while watching for overthrows in foul territory to the right (see pictures 8-1 and 8-2). Turning to the left puts the runner in danger of being tagged out, but as long as the runner stays straight (or veers off slightly to the right), they may safely walk straight back to first base if the umpire has called them safe.

I'm often asked about whether runners should slide into first base on close plays. I do not want my runners sliding into first base. I cannot emphasize this enough. It may look cool or exciting, but the risk far outweighs the reward. Sliding into first base is almost always slower, and puts players at far greater risk of an injury to the hands, arms, shoulder, neck, head, etc. The only situation when sliding into first *may* be smart to consider is if an errant throw pulls the first baseman off the bag and into the runner's path and by sliding, the runner may be able to avoid the tag.

On clear base hits to the outfield (except those to short right field) or balls hit in the air to the outfield, the batter-runner should create an angle so that they are in better position to go to second base. To do this, the batter-runner runs straight for a few steps out of the box, and then takes an arc outside the baseline. They should touch the inside corner of first base (with either foot) and locate the ball to see if they can make it to second (see pictures 8-3, 8-4 and 8-5). When the runner determines they cannot get to second base safely (keeping their head up and listening to the first base coach), they should then slow their body down, and return to first base. If the decision is to try for second base, they simply continue running hard on the angled path they've created.

8-3: On clear base hits to the outfield, batters should take an aggressive turn at first base in case they have an opportunity to advance to second base

8-4: On clear base hits to the outfield, batters should take an aggressive turn at first base and look for the ball and listen for the first base coach's instructions

8-5: Several steps past the base, the batter should prepare to head back to first base unless they can see the ball has gotten away from the outfielder or the first base coach tells them to go for second

On First Base—Taking a Lead

With younger age groups, taking leads and stealing bases is typically not permitted in order to simplify the game. As players advance, however, they will reach a level of the game that more closely resembles the big leagues and understanding leading and base stealing will become necessary.

When a runner safely reaches first base the first thing he should do *before* taking his *primary* lead (and while still on the base) is get the signs from the third base coach. Once they've done this, they're ready to take a lead. They should face the pitcher and shuffle their feet as opposed to walking off the bag, keeping their eyes on the pitcher all of the time (as in 100 percent). Starting from the back corner of the base, they should try to stay balanced without touching or crossing their feet. A lead of about 2–3 stride lengths is normal, but a rule of thumb should be that in case of a pick-off attempt from the pitcher, the base runner can just return to the base with a quick step and a dive (see pictures 8-6, 8-7 and 8-8). As players reach higher levels of the game and develop a greater awareness of the game (pitcher's tendencies, catcher's throwing arm, game situation, etc.), they will adjust their leads accordingly.

Once the runner has taken their lead, they should stay balanced with their eyes on the *lower* half of the pitcher's body. Runners should never take their eyes away from this target, even as they are taking their

8-6: At first base, baserunners should take a lead of 2- 3 stride lengths without crossing or touching their feet together

8-7: At first base, baserunners should take a lead of 2- 3 stride lengths without crossing or touching their feet together

8-8: At first base, baserunners should take a lead of 2- 3 stride lengths without crossing or touching their feet together

lead. Once the pitcher throws to the plate, the runner should take a *secondary* lead where they take two more shuffles toward second base. They should be in an athletic position (knees slightly bent, hands out in front), and land on their second shuffle as the ball crosses home plate. If the pitcher throws over to first, the runner should take a hard step with their right foot back across their body and dive for the back corner of the base, making it difficult for the first baseman to tag them (see picture 8-9). If the pickoff attempt is slow, the runner may return to first base standing up. (One safety note here—the runner should turn their head toward first base—away from the pitcher—as they are going back to avoid an errant throw hitting them in the face).

8-9: Baserunners should dive towards the back corner of first base on a pickoff attempt with heads up looking to see if the ball got past the first baseman

On First Base—Steal Situation

When the runner has been given the steal sign, they should keep these same guidelines in mind. They should not lean their weight on either foot or guess what the pitcher will do. The base runner should take a normal length lead and keep their weight balanced so as not to alert the pitcher of their intent to steal second. Finally, they should stay athletic and simply react to what they see from the pitcher.

Once the base runner reads that the pitcher is throwing to the plate, their first movement should be a strong crossover step with his left foot. Players should stay low for the first few steps, drive their knees and arms, and gradually rise into a more upright sprinting position. It is also important to be alert to the result of the pitch. I teach my runners to "peek" in toward home plate when they are about halfway to second as the ball enters the hitting zone. The runner then can react accordingly if the batter swings and makes contact. If not, then they continue running hard toward second base.

When sliding, players should practice the pop-up slide, as it is both effective and safe. While there is an element of the headfirst slide that makes it fun to watch, going in with your head is potentially more dangerous (much greater risk of injury) and usually no quicker than a feet-first slide. On a pop-up slide, players should form a "4" with their legs. One leg should be extended (the one that will contact second base) while the other leg should be bent with the foot tucked under the hamstring of the leg being extended. The hands should be kept up in the air instead of bracing the slide (see picture 8-10); many professional players hold their batting gloves in their hands while on the base paths, which can provide a simple reminder to keep the hands off the ground. Players should maintain their speed and allow the momentum of their slide to propel them back to a standing position.

8-10: On a pop-up slide, players should form a "4" with their legs, with one leg extended and the other leg bent and their arms up

When a hit and run play is on, base runners do not need to place *as much* emphasis on taking a large lead or getting a great jump. However, aside from these two things, runners should treat a hit and run exactly like a steal attempt and run hard in case the batter swings and misses or misses the sign the coach has given. Players should *never* get picked off on a hit and run, as they can and should sacrifice a good jump based on the assumption (and hope) that the batter will make contact with the pitch. After crossing over and taking a few strides, again the runner should peek in to home plate to find the ball and react to what they see.

If a right-handed pitcher is on the mound, runners really only need to pay attention to the pitcher's feet. If the pitcher's right foot moves first, thereby indicating a pickoff attempt, the runner should get back to first. However, if the pitcher's left foot moves first, the pitcher must make a pitch to the plate or be charged with a balk.

Left-handers are trickier to read because they can hang their front leg up in the air and still have the option of pitching the ball or throwing over to first base. Runners will learn to judge lefties and should keep in mind that they have to step at a 45° angle or greater—in relation to home plate and first base—if they want to throw to first. In other words, the pitcher's leg must land at an angle closer to first base than home plate when the pitcher is throwing over to first base. If the pitcher steps at an angle closer to home plate while attempting a pickoff, it is a balk. Another indicator that a left-handed pitcher is throwing a pitch to the plate is that the runner will see the upper half of the pitcher's body lean toward home plate. Once this "lean" is observed, the runner knows the pitcher cannot attempt a pickoff at first.

On First Base

If a runner is on first base and there is a routine fly ball with less than two outs, players should go as far as they can on the base path to second base without losing the ability to get back to first base safely in case the ball is caught. In doing so, they give themselves the best chance possible of advancing to second (or further) safely in case the ball is not caught. On longer fly balls (that should be playable by the outfielder) where a runner knows that they can *tag up* (return to the base and attempt to advance once the ball is caught), they should do so. If a runner is unsure about whether or not they should tag, they should always err on the side of caution and tag up anyway (and remember to listen for your first base coach). Even if they know they will not try to advance, they can take a few hard steps as if they are going to in order to force the outfielder to make a quick throw in to second. The throw may be errant, and the runners will be able to advance. On pop-ups and fly balls in foul territory, players should always tag up in case the ball is caught and is deep enough to advance, or if the fielder is not in a good position to make a strong throw to second.

On ground balls in the infield, runners should always run hard to second and try to break up a potential double play. To do this, they should slide normally straight into second base. Base runners should not veer out of the base path or slide past the base in order to obstruct the fielder. Many leagues have rules against this type of obstruction as it may lead to an injury of either the fielder or the runner. (Players should know and follow whatever safe sliding guidelines their local leagues have in their rules).

The only time players should not run hard to second on a ground ball is if the ball is hit slow enough to the second baseman such that a good second baseman will try to tag the runner and then throw to first. To prevent this, players should stop so that the second baseman cannot tag them.

On base hits to the outfield, runners should "round" second base, picking up the third base coach right after they hit the base. They should create an angle (arc slightly out toward the outfield) from first base so that they can hit the inside part of second base, and head in a straight line to third base.

When a batter hits a line drive, all base runners should freeze, as they may need to quickly return to the base, if the ball is caught, to avoid a double play. If the ball gets through the infield, the runners should have enough time to reach the next base even if they initially freeze.

Although it may be difficult to at first remember all the different scenarios mentioned above (and variations of these as well), coaches should spend ample time in practice to give players enough experience to be able to make good base running decisions. Additionally, a good first base coach will let base runners know what they need to be ready for. Base coaches (who are paying attention and not on their cell phones!) can see everything that is going on, so they should be utilized as such.

On Second Base

Before getting the signs from the third base coach, runners on second base should briefly turn around and check the positioning of the outfielders to help make decisions on balls hit in play. This is especially important on *fly* balls because if players can advance to third base by tagging up, once on third base, a base runner is only a wild pitch, a passed ball, or if there are less than 2 outs, a fly ball away from scoring a run. Base runners can typically take a slightly longer primary and secondary lead from second base because there is *usually* nobody closely holding them on. At lower levels of the game, however, some teams tend to have the shortstop or the second baseman hovering near the base until the pitch is thrown. In this case, the base runner should shorten their lead to make sure they can get back in case a pickoff attempt is made.

On leads with less than two outs, base runners should take a lead just as they would on first base, *directly* in line with third. Runners should keep their feet moving in place ("chop their feet" is a phrase frequently associated with this) and listen to the third base coach if they need to lengthen or shorten up their lead.

With two outs, players should take a deeper lead back towards the shortstop (see pictures 8-11 through 8-14). By doing so, this allows players to create the angle they need to round third base and score on a base hit. Runners also do this with two outs because they are generally running on any hit ball.

8-11: Getting a proper lead at second base with two outs

8-12: Getting a proper lead at second base with two outs

8-13: Getting a proper lead at second base with two outs

8-14: Getting a proper lead at second base with two outs

If a base runner is on second with less than two outs, and there is nobody on first, the runner has a choice of whether to run or hold up on a ground ball hit on the infield. A rule of thumb is if the ball is to the base runner's right (to the left side of the infield), they should hold but if it is at them or to the base runner's left, they should go to third. (An exception: on a slow roller to the left side of the infield and not close to the third base bag, the base runner may well be able to safely advance to third base.) As runners approach third base, they should again pick up their base coach and listen for instructions. As always, they should be aggressive and be ready to take advantage of a defensive mistake that would allow them to take an extra base.

On Third Base

Leading off third base is slightly different than that of first or second. Players should take two steps directly back off third base into foul territory and then take a few steps down the line towards home plate. If a base runner is hit in fair territory by a batted ball, they are ruled out. As a result, taking a lead in *foul* territory off of third base ensures the runner will not be called out on a bat-ted ball that hits them. As the pitcher winds up and the pitch is being thrown, the base runner should turn their bodies towards home and walk slowly forward in a crouched position taking three steps. They should step with their right foot, then the left, and finally the right again just as the ball crosses home plate, ready to head for home in case the ball gets by the catcher. If a pitch ends up in the catcher's glove, the runner should retreat back to third base. In returning back to third, the runner should go back in *fair* territory (right on the baseline) making it difficult for the catcher to try and throw back to pick them off (see pictures 8-15 through 8-18).

8-15: Baserunners should take their lead off third base in foul territory, but return back to the bag in fair territory

8-16: Baserunners should take their lead off third base in foul territory, but return back to the bag in fair territory

8-17: Baserunners should take their lead off third base in foul territory, but return back to the bag in fair territory

8-18: Baserunners should take their lead off third base in foul territory, but return back to the bag in fair territory

On routine fly balls with less than two outs, players should immediately get back to the base and tag up. As soon as the ball is caught, the player can sprint home if they can score before the fielders can get the ball to the plate. The third base coach should be communicating to the runner to go or to stay put.

On deeper fly balls, runners should always tag up as well because if the ball is caught, they can score easily, and if the ball is not caught, they will again have plenty of time to score (see picture 8-19). In addition to using their own judgment and instinct, the base runner should listen for the third base coach's instructions. Sometimes the game situation will dictate whether a runner tries to score or not when it appears that it will be a close play at the plate.

8-19: Tagging up on a fly ball at third base

Finally, when a base runner scores, if there is another runner(s) heading home on the same play, the first runner to score should stand near the plate (but out of the way) to help communicate to the other runner(s). They must be in a position where they won't interfere with a play at the plate and should both motion with their hands and yell for their teammate to either slide or stand up. In either case, the base runner should never attempt to collide with the catcher—the general rule is to slide or avoid contact. These rules are on the books in youth leagues to help avoid injuries and are in place now at higher levels of the game include major league baseball.

Practicing Baserunning

Coaches should incorporate base running situations into most practices. This practice should be done at "game speed" rather than simply having the players go through the motions. Learning the nuances of base running through experience and repetition will give your players an opportunity to succeed when the game is on the line.

Two ways to run to first base are important - most kids don't know how to run properly to first base. The first way to practice is to run through first base, hitting the front of the base at full speed. The second way is to work at rounding the bag—"banana out."

Here's a base running drill that I really like. Divide your team into two lines at home plate and when you yell "go" have players run one at a time from each line doing the following:

Line One: Run hard through first base. Next, the runner on first base runs to third base. Then, the player on third base tags up and runs home.

Line Two: Run from home to second base. Next, runner on second base runs home.

The next players in the two lines don't go until the prior runners have gotten to their appropriate bases, have had about 15 seconds to catch their breath, and the coach yells out "go." This drill teaches players how to run bases and gets players some needed fitness.

Chapter 9

Becoming the Best Baseball Player You Are Capable of Being

This book is about educating coaches and parents so that you can help your kids make the most of their talents and continually learn and grow as baseball players. It's important for parents and coaches to understand that the focus should be on kids becoming the best baseball players that they are capable of becoming rather than making comparisons between the development of their kids and those around them. Making the most of your talents and developing them to the best extent possible has nothing to do with competing with others to win starting spots or college scholarships, and everything to do with being a better player than you were yesterday.

Striving to be the best they can be and learning to be part of a team will help young athletes in all aspects of their lives—in school, future jobs, personal relationships, etc. Learning to excel at a sport while balancing other responsibilities also helps young players learn important time management skills.

To help focus on becoming a more complete baseball player, young athletes should consider that baseball coaches and scouts at the college level and beyond generally evaluate a baseball player by considering five main aspects of a young player's game, or "tools." These five tools for position players (non-pitchers) are: arm strength, fielding ability, the ability to hit for average, hitting for power and running speed. Some of the very best professional baseball players are known as "five tool players" because they excel in all five of these categories (there aren't many truly five-tool players). In this respect, it's important for young ballplayers and their coaches to evaluate themselves as honestly as possible in order to determine what areas of their game need the most work and train accordingly.

In addition to these physical characteristics, scouts are also interested in a prospect's "makeup" or his attitude towards the game. College baseball coaches and major league organizations seek players that bring energy and a positive attitude to the ballpark every day; they are looking for players who will be able to deal with adversity and continue to strive to reach their full potential, because the reality is that when a player is recruited for college or drafted into the pros, he is far from a finished product. It is not uncommon for even the best college and high school players who are drafted to struggle when they first enter the minor leagues (also known as affiliated ball). Scouts need to find players who will be willing to work through these struggles and ultimately become better ballplayers than they were when they first came out of school.

⊘ ⊘ ⊘ ⊘ ⊘ ⊘ ⊘ **Story from Dan** ⊘ ⊘ ⊘ ⊘ ⊘ ⊘ ⊘

Colin Moran, who played under me from ages 10-15, isn't a great athlete but really developed himself and has a high baseball IQ. He had a willingness to develop his full potential and be the best player he could be. Talentwise, I've had better kids, but he has an outstanding work ethic. He makes himself a better player every year. His high baseball IQ comes from attentiveness and learning from experience. He would never make the same mistake twice, he learned the first time that he made a certain mistake. He expected a lot from himself, so you didn't need to say a lot to him.

Coaches need to monitor how hard players are on themselves. It didn't work to yell at Colin because he was already hard on himself. He needed to learn to let things go—you can't let things fester and expect to perform well as a baseball player.

Developing Your Full Potential

So, what should young players do to reach their full potential? First of all, it's important that they work on skills outside of team organized practices and games. During the course of a season, coaches simply do not have the time to work with players on their individual skills every day. They need to work on more team-oriented concepts such as bunt defense or pick off plays so that the team as a whole can be successful. This is not to say that a player cannot improve his hitting or fielding over the course of a season, however, it is important for kids to realize that they must take it upon themselves to work on the things that they need to improve upon in their own free time.

That being said, balance in life is important and youth ballplayers should be careful not to over-train. Days off can be a good thing—they refresh your body and your passion for the game. Sometimes what a player does to recover, whether it be taking days off, sleeping enough or eating regularly and right, can be just as important as what he's doing in the batting cage.

As an aside, playing a sport should never prevent or provide an athlete with an excuse for not doing the best that they can in their classes. Whether one decides to stop playing baseball in high school or has a long professional career, it's important for young ballplayers to recognize that their playing days will not last forever. What a kid learns in the classroom and throughout their years of schooling will play a major role in what type of work they will ultimately take on after they hang up their cleats, and for this reason, it's important to get a good education.

Working on the Five Tools

In terms of tools, arm strength is fairly simple to work on. Players should try to long-toss a couple times a week (see Chapter 10 for a description of long toss). In addition to long-tossing, when playing catch, players focus on using their whole body to ensure that every throw is crisp. Especially in the early teenage years, players typically see a decent jump in their throwing velocity as they become bigger and stronger.

Long-tossing and strengthening the entire body will help players throw the ball even harder as they continue to grow and develop.

Working on fielding ability is also fairly straightforward. In my opinion, the two factors that contribute the most to how well a ballplayer fields his position are athleticism and repetition. While a player's general level of athleticism is not completely within their control, how hard they choose to work is entirely up to them. Major league infielders can make spectacular plays look routine because they have made that play thousands of times before in practice. Infielders and outfielders should try to find someone to hit them ground balls or fly balls whenever possible. Infielders can always work on their footwork, transfers and throws to first base and outfielders can work on their crow hops and taking good routes to balls. Catchers can work on blocking balls, receiving, framing and making throws to bases. There are many different ways for kids to improve their defense, but nearly all of them require practice and game-speed repetitions.

The two hitting tools: hitting for power and hitting for average, can be developed through deliberate practice and hard work as well. Drills that I like to do on a regular basis are tee work, front toss and regular batting practice. While front toss or batting practice requires a second person, players can work on their swing on a batting tee all by themselves.

In terms of hitting development, it is important to remember that hitting a baseball is one of the hardest things in the world. Especially when making adjustments to the swing, it is common for players to feel uncomfortable as they try to retrain their body to move differently. It is important to keep in mind that developing the swing is an ongoing process, and that improvement over time is the goal, not immediate success.

Hitting for average is largely a function of hand-eye coordination and swing mechanics. While a solid, efficient swing will put players in a position to get to balls, having good hand-eye coordination will allow them to make consistent contact and hit for average.

Hitting for power is much of the same and also takes into account how strong and powerful the batter is. It is also important for hitters to be good athletes. Once players get to the high school level, they can begin to work at weight training to strengthen their entire body which can help them hit for more power. Refining swing mechanics should also help players hit balls harder more consistently. In my opinion, these two tools can sometimes be the toughest to develop.

Finally, in order to get faster, players need to run sprints and get stronger. Some kids make the mistake of running distance (miles) in order to get faster, but in order to improve sprinting speed, the body must be trained to run fast. 30- and 60-yard sprints are the most practical for ballplayers (the respective distances from home to first and home to second) and should be done with maximum effort. Strengthening the body will also play a large role in helping players to become faster as well as developing a quicker, more powerful first step.

Developing Team Skills

Aside from physical skills, it's important for young ballplayers to remember to be a good teammate and to bring energy to every practice and game that they participate in. Regardless of how a player personally is performing in a game, it doesn't take any talent to hustle on and off the field or support a teammate. While these things are not quantifiable like the velocity of a pitcher's fastball or a shortstop's 60-yard dash time, they also play a large role in how successful a player and his team will be. By working hard to become a better ballplayer and a better teammate, players should ultimately see results in their team's performance and in the type of person they will become.

Chapter 10

Coaching Clinic

Developing good habits in practice is extremely important and will play a large role in what type of ballplayer a kid will develop into. By training the right movements at game speed in practice, ideally kids will be able to more consistently field ground balls correctly and hit hard line drives at the plate in the game without much thinking—because they have intentionally trained these movements so many times before in practice.

As a coach, it is critical that you work hard to teach kids the fundamentals, but at the same time, keep them active and moving in order to keep them engaged. Especially with younger kids, the number one thing that they want to do is move. Utilizing small groups and keeping practices of reasonable length (more on that in a moment) will serve to maximize how much your kids will get out of a team practice and also will prevent them from getting bored. An efficient, productive team practice should maximize the allotted field space, time available, and capabilities of both coaches and players. The goal is to create a practice environment that will reinforce solid fundamentals in order to allow each player to feel confident and relaxed in game situations.

Proper Practice Gear

It might sound silly but make sure your kids know what to wear to practice. Make sure that they wear a baseball hat and baseball pants.

Some teams have practice jerseys or shirts. If you want, have your kids tuck their shirts in. The idea is that you want them to look like ballplayers preparing for game-like conditions.

Especially when kids get older, some teams will allow their players to practice in shorts. For younger kids though, many of them like to slide. They want to dive for balls and slide into bases and get dirty. Encourage this! It's better for them to be wearing baseball pants when they do these things.

Length of Practices

The ideal amount of time for a team practice is somewhere between 1 and 2 hours. An hour and a half for practice is pretty standard and is, in my opinion, a pretty good length of time for a practice. However, coaches must remember to use their common sense. If this is a tee-ball team of 6-year olds, kids likely do not want to hear their coaches talk to them about hitting mechanics for an hour, whereas players on a high school team would probably struggle to improve if they are practicing as a team for just one hour at a time. As players get older, their attention spans will grow which will allow you to spend more time on areas of the game that may be perceived as boring by younger players.

As a coach, you also have to stay in tune with how your players are feeling. If your team just came back from a tournament in which your team played five games in 48 hours, you should give your team a day or two off and not be having them long-toss or doing other throwing-intensive drills the next day back in practice. This is just not good for their arms. Furthermore, try to stay away from drills that are too complicated or difficult for the age group of kids that you are coaching. As a coach, you need to seek feedback from the group about how well your practices are being run. Usually, the body language of your players will tell you a lot about this.

Typical Team Practice

So, what does a typical team practice actually look like? First of all, beginning each practice with a short five to ten-minute active warm-up is a must. As opposed to static stretching, getting your players moving with movements like lunges, high-knees or shuffles can help warm up their muscles, improve blood circulation, activate the central nervous system, and minimize the risk of injury. In short, starting practice off with an active warm-up (one that also can be done before a game) will allow your players to perform their best and hopefully will cause them to get injured less frequently.

Afterwards, the team should transition into receiving and throwing, or in other words, playing catch. This portion of practice is frequently mis-used with kids lazily tossing the ball back and forth with their partner, with no real purpose other than just "warming up." While you are get-ting your arm loose by playing catch, the intent and purpose of playing catch each day should be to get better! Defensively, the basis of baseball is throwing and catching the ball. When playing catch, players need to be working on their footwork, their transfers (transferring the ball from their glove to their throwing hand) and throwing to their partner chest-high with each throw. Throwing should last about 10–15 minutes.

As I describe in the nearby sidebar, you can also implement a point system for your team's throwing in order to make things more compet-itive and keep the kids focused. Coaches should also try to have their kids long toss at least once a week. By long toss, I mean starting out close together and stretching it out until your throwing partner is at a distance that is tough to reach even when using a crow hop. This drill is great for helping your players to improve their arm strength and is also usually a lot of fun for kids.

The next portion of your practice will usually depend on how many coaches you have available. If you are lucky enough to have three coaches or even just two, you can split up into groups and work on dif-

⊘ ⊘ ⊘ ⊘ ⊘ ⊘ ⊘ **Story from Dan** ⊘ ⊘ ⊘ ⊘ ⊘ ⊘ ⊘
Competition in Practice Drills

One way to make practices more fun is to turn drills into competitions. For example, instead of just telling kids to play catch, incorporate a point system to your team's daily throwing routine. Give kids two points for a throw to the face and one point for a throw to their throwing partner's chest and see who can get to 21 first. Or during batting practice, reward hitters for line drives in the gap or hard-hit balls up the middle. Anytime you can get your kids to compete it will make them more engaged, more invested, and more focused on the task at hand.

At the same time, it's important to remember that especially with younger ballplayers, we don't want competition in practice to discourage kids from playing the game. For example, continually pitting stronger players against weaker players in competitive drills can serve to destroy a weaker player's self-esteem. At the end of the day, your job as the coach is to provide an environment where all of your players can improve upon their skills and have a positive playing experience. While it can be helpful to implement competitions in a practice setting in order to keep kids engaged, coaches should use their judgment and recognize the fact that some weaker players will be less excited about competing with their teammates in practice and proceed accordingly.

ferent things. Ideally, you will be able to split up outfielders, infielders and pitchers (catchers sometimes might work with infielders and at other times with pitchers). Station work should last about 15–20 minutes and will allow you to get a lot more done than just having 15 guys standing around while one player at a time hits batting practice. Infielders can work on double play feeds, do footwork drills or could use flat gloves to work on their hands fielding ground balls. With older players, you can even split up and have middle infielders do double-play flips while corner guys work on fielding slow rollers. With younger guys, you can work on relays and cutoffs (this can actually be done with the outfielders as well and is great to work on if you don't have many other coaches available). If you have the ability to, split the catchers up into their own group and have them work on blocking, receiving and their footwork.

Outfielders can work on their crow hops, and their communication by hitting two lines of outfielders fly balls that fall somewhere in between them. You should also sometimes have outfielders practice their footwork through drop steps and catching fly balls that they have to catch over their shoulder.

Pitchers should work on their mechanics and if guys need to throw bullpens, let them do so with catchers. Hitting drills can be incorporated into station work however you see fit. If you want to have one group of three to four kids hit off a tee while three to four others take live batting practice and three to four others shag balls, this usually works well.

After this, you will usually have about 30–40 minutes left of practice to spend however you see fit. This time is frequently used for team defense, fielding work and base running. In season, you should try to work on things that your team needs to improve upon. If in the last game a couple pop ups dropped in between an outfielder and infielder, work on communication and catching those types of fly balls. If your team misplayed a sacrifice bunt, work on bunt defense.

Use your outfielders as base runners as your infielders, pitchers and catchers rotate through various game situations. If you want, you can also use this time to run a controlled scrimmage. This allows guys to get three to four at bats off of live pitching and allows you to step in and coach when you need to. This is something that is also good to do if you have pitchers who have not pitched in a game recently but need to get some pitching work in.

Overall, the goal is to run an active, fast-moving practice. You want your guys to come out of practice feeling good about the fact that they worked hard to improve themselves as players. How you use your practice time during the season will play a huge role in how your players master skills and how well your club performs come game time.

Here's how a typical practice from 3:00 to 4:30 P.M. might look:

3:00–3:05   Active Warm-up

3:05–3:15   Throw/Long-Toss

3:15–3:30   Defensive Stations

(Infielders → double play feeds, outfielders → communication drills, catchers → blocking and receiving and pitchers → work on mechanics

3:30–3:50   Hitting Stations (use resources available – e.g. screens, hitting tees, etc.)

(Split up into four groups: Group 1 → Tee work, Group 2 → Front Toss, Group 3 → Live Batting Practice, Group 4 → Bunting)

3:50–4:30   Controlled Scrimmage – break the team into two smaller teams (e.g. six players each, with shared pitchers and catchers). Coach periodically steps in and explains situations and responsibilities at key points during play.

Instilling Confidence

Last but not least, I'd like to briefly highlight the importance of instilling confidence in your players. This will enable them to relax and maximize their ability to perform up to their potential. Coaches should strive to create an environment where players can be relaxed, have fun and work hard without risk of being yelled at or humiliated if they make a mistake. Strive to find the balance between recognizing when a player or the team's game needs improvement while emphasizing their strengths and giving positive feedback.

Appendix

Rules and Customs

At the highest levels of baseball there are thousands of rules, many of which never even get used over the course of a team's season. The rules of the game may differ among age groups and levels of play, but in general they attempt to promote simplicity, efficient games, a better instructional environment, and player safety.

What follows are the most basic rules for a fundamental understanding of the game.

The Game

In a game of baseball, two teams of nine players in the game at a time alternate between offense (batting and attempting to score runs) and defense (playing the field and trying to stop the other team from scoring). At the younger ages, extra players are often allowed in the batting order; it is not uncommon to see very young teams batting 11 or 12 players in their lineups. Some leagues for younger players may also allow more than nine players on defense—for example, having four outfielders instead of three. I prefer to see reasonably sized teams at the younger levels so that you can bat as close to nine or ten players as possible and play with nine in the field. As it is, baseball is a game with very little action compared to most other sports so it is important to keep kids engaged in the game. The more at bats each player gets and the more times he touches the ball in the field, the more opportunities there are for development and learning and the more enjoyable the game should be for those players.

Games can often be started with a minimum of eight players on either team at lower levels but no less. Games at the younger youth levels will generally last either six or seven innings, and older travel teams may choose to play a nine inning game instead of a doubleheader.

To start with the very basics of baseball, the team that scores more runs during the game wins. Runs are scored by completing a counterclockwise circuit around the four bases. In some younger leagues and opening rounds of some travel tournaments, if both teams have the same number of runs after the scheduled number of innings, the game will end in a tie. However, in most leagues, the game will continue until after a full inning, one team has more runs than the other.

Offense

While at-bat, or on offense, a team tries to score runs by having runners touch each of the four bases (running counter clockwise around them) before three outs are recorded in an inning. The nine starting players (at lower levels extra hitters that do not play the field can sometimes be added on to the nine) on the offensive team hit in a batting order although substitutions can be made throughout the game. Once substituted out of a game at the Major League level, players cannot re-enter the game, but at the youth level, they oftentimes are allowed to be substituted back into the game in their prior spot in the batting order. An at-bat will continue until a batter either makes an out or gets on base. During an at-bat, if a batter records three strikes he is considered out. A strike is called when either the batter swings and misses on a pitched ball, makes contact with a ball that doesn't go in the field of play, or the ball passes through the strike zone and the player does not offer a swing. (An at bat can continue on a fouled ball with two-strikes so long as the ball wasn't bunted in which case that is a strikeout.)

By its most current definition, the strike zone is the space over home plate between the bottom of the batter's knees and their chest (where the letters generally are on their uniform top). If a batter records four balls, they have walked, and can freely proceed to first base. A ball is any pitch out of the strike zone at which the batter does offer a swing at. Due to the difficulty of throwing strikes at younger age levels, umpires generally allow for a slightly larger strike zone the younger the players in a given league.

Defense

In the field, or on defense, a team tries to record three outs while preventing the offensive team from scoring runs. There are nine different positions on the field. The infield consists of the pitcher (who throws pitches to the batters), the catcher (catches pitches from the pitcher that are not hit), the first baseman, the second baseman, the shortstop, and the third baseman who occupy different areas of the infield. The outfield consists of the right fielder, center fielder, and left fielder. While generally not used among players on younger baseball teams, sometimes a team will utilize a designated hitter, or DH, who does not play the field, but hits for one of the fielders (usually the pitcher) in the batting order.

There are a number of ways to record outs on defense. One is a strike-out, or when an out occurs because a batter accumulates three strikes. Infield ground outs occur when a fielder fields a ground ball and throws it to the first baseman who steps on the first base before the batter reaches that base. Another way to record an out is a force out, a play in which a runner who is forced to run to the next base (because a runner occupies the base previous to the one he occupies) fails to reach it before a fielder steps on that base while in possession of the ball. For example, if there's a runner on first and the batter hits a ground ball to the shortstop who throws the ball to the second baseman who is covering and standing on second base, and the ball gets there before the base runner gets there, he is forced out.

Tag outs occur when a fielder touches a runner not occupying a base either with the ball or with his glove with the ball in it. A final way to record an out on defense is via a fly out. This is when a batted ball is caught while in flight, before it has touched the ground (or fence). Recording outs are not limited to these methods, though they are the most common.

Advanced Concepts

Here are some slightly more advanced concepts of which younger players should be aware:

Tagging up—With less than two outs and on a ball hit in the air, runners must either remain on the base that they were occupying on the pitch, or return to it and "tag up"—touch it after a fielder has caught the ball. Coaches should remind runners that it does not matter if a fielder bobbles the ball, as soon as the fielder touches it then the runner is free to leave. Additionally, players should know that they need to locate the ball, even on steal attempts, or they may easily get doubled off.

Dropped third strikes—Most youth baseball leagues allow batters to run to first base on dropped third strikes. At high school, college, and basically all higher levels of baseball, a third strike that the catcher does not receive cleanly is a dropped third strike. If first base is occupied with less than two outs, the batter is out, but if there are two outs or first base is unoccupied, the batter needs to be tagged out or forced out at first. Remind runners that they can advance if they choose to, but obviously don't have to if first base is occupied with less than two outs. Also remind catchers to create a throwing lane to first on these plays and to not try to throw over the runner. Catchers should also know that if the bases are loaded on a dropped third strike with two outs, they can simply step on home plate for the force out.

Dead ball vs. live ball—This could refer to the baseball era in the early 1900's where there were very few home runs but in this context, dead ball refers to any situation where the ball is not in play. When an umpire throws up his hands after a foul ball, he is indicating this situation. At younger levels of baseball where taking leads is prohibited, after the pitcher receives the ball back from the catcher the ball is considered dead and runners must return to the base they are occupying. At any level where leading is allowed, this is not the case. When the pitcher has the ball and the umpire has not called for time, runners are free to advance or be tagged out if not on a base. When kids make the transition from dead ball to live ball situations, pitchers need to be instructed on pickoffs and balks, and runners need instruction on leading.

The strike zone—Although it is defined in the official rule book, this will differ somewhat depending on the level of play and the individual umpire. At the younger levels, you will obviously have the least parity among umpires—they are not professionals at their job, just the same as players. Some will call strikes at kids' chests, at their ankles, three to six inches off the outside corner, on balls the catcher misses, and everything in between.

At the end of the day, the strike zone is what the umpire dictates. This cannot be overemphasized to players, coaches, and spectators. The strike zone is one of the least acceptable topics to argue with umpires because other than the batter and catcher, nobody else really has a great view. Umpires are mostly consistent between teams but there will always be bad calls. Pay attention early in the game to see what pitches the umpire is and is not calling for strikes. After the first inning, if you've watched every at bat, you should have a good idea. The best thing to do is to avoid fixating on the ump and focus on what you personally can control. As MLB manager and former catcher Mike Matheny would say, this means that players should focus on playing the game, coaches should focus on coaching the game and spectators should focus on watching the game.

Matheny enjoyed a playing career where he was recognized as an elite defensive catcher of his time. Shortly after his retirement, he agreed to coach a little league team, granted that he do it on his own terms. He wrote a letter to the parents of his players which has since gone viral—dubbed a manifesto of sorts for sports parenting—detailing his expectations for them and their children. He promised to get as much out of the kids' ability as he possibly could, provided that the parents bought into his system and approach. While he does encourage parents to spend time practicing with their kids outside of team practices, he believes they should refrain from yelling anything in the stands and only act as a "silent, constant, source of support." Loud cheering certainly feels like it helps your kid and his teammates or maybe it just helps you to feel involved. Regardless, Matheny argues that despite positive intentions, this only adds unnecessary pressure to the kids—impeding their development and enjoyment of the game. If you've ever been to a youth game, you know that persuading an entire group of fans to buy into this philosophy is nearly impossible. Maybe you yourself as a parent cannot adhere to this as again, it is a fairly radical philosophy (hence the attention it received). However, these are some practices that should be avoided at all costs:

Cheering excessively—This obviously doesn't break any rules but can really create a negative atmosphere. Some might construe this as being "intense" or "into the game," but it simply makes the game harder for other fans to watch or to focus as a player. Trust me, you aren't doing anybody any favors in life by reminding the pitcher how many home runs your youngster has hit off of other pre-pubescent hurlers in the past three tournaments on fields the size of your backyard. Sit back and enjoy the game. If you really can't help yourself, then keep a scorebook, but embarrassing your son, his team, and yourself by rooting too hard is definitely a no-no.

Being verbally abusive—This is even less acceptable and well-intentioned than the previous issue of excessive cheering. The most common target of abuse is umpires, but you will see cases where fans try to help their team by insulting or trying to rattle the other team and their coaches. It's one thing to heckle the players on the field at a major league stadium, but it's quite another to tear down a kid, his youth team and coaches. No game is so important that winning it at the cost of insulting the other team's pitcher and/or his father, no matter how much you dislike them. If you wouldn't say it at the office or in front of your friends, then don't say it at the field.

Interfering with play—This idea applies much less at younger levels. Every once in a while, you'll see someone fall out of the stands at an MLB game while flailing at a ball down the line. If you do this, at least at a professional game, you will probably be kicked out and likely not get to keep the ball if you did happen to grab it. You are also potentially affecting the outcome of the game by interfering with balls that are still in play. If your kid hits his first ever homerun and you want to chase after it in the woods then have at it. But if the ball is in play then leave it alone. Keep this in mind, especially when choosing a place to sit or stand along the sidelines. If you aren't clear about where you may watch the game, ask a nearby umpire. And, always respect and listen to umpires who may try to explain that you need to move because you could be in the way where you are.

A side note for coaches: your behavior is the model that many parents will follow. Being out of control and screaming at umps will give implicit permission to the parents to do the same, just as being civilized will generally compel them to follow as well. Keep it a positive experience for everyone involved. Remember, you lead by example, not just by what you say.

Understanding Customs: The "Unwritten Rules"

Baseball is a game steeped in tradition and culture. America's favorite pastime has numerous customs that aren't discussed anywhere in the rule book but have developed over the decades in countries worldwide. Here are some to know:

Picking up teammates—This could refer to two different practices. The first concerns players on the bench standing up and giving their teammates high-fives, fist-bumps, and general encouragement for doing something good. This obviously isn't required but is most applicable when a pitcher is removed from game. If you're too lazy to congratulate anyone otherwise, this is the one time to do it. The other application is when players are stranded on base and their teammates bring their gloves and hats to them so they don't have to come back in to the dugout to pick them up themselves before taking the field on defense. Stranded runners will give their helmet and maybe their batting gloves to either the first or third base coach to take in and wait for their gear from their teammates. This becomes more prevalent in higher levels of baseball. Infielders pick up infielders (as they're going to the same place) and outfielders pick up outfielders though conceivably bench players could take care of this responsibility. It is just more efficient if players who are already going out to the field carry out this duty. Both practices of "picking up teammates" can promote positivism and team unity.

Showing up the umpire—Arguing definitely falls into this category but even subtle, disrespectful gestures can earn an umpire's disapproval and potentially cost your team some calls down the road. This includes, but isn't limited to: making faces, bad body language, throwing things, and anticipating a walk and leaving before the umpire calls ball four. Catchers in particular should be sure to respect umpires because they have the opportunity to establish a relationship with them—either good or bad. You'd think twice about giving a long look after taking a called third strike if you remembered you had five more innings to go behind the plate with an angry ump at your back. Again, they are human beings too. Nobody wants to be embarrassed or look bad on a ball field, umpires are just the same.

Showboating—Baseball occupies the low end of the spectrum in the sports world in terms of tolerance for this practice. Some examples are bat-flipping, jogging too slowly around the bases after a homer or down to first on a walk, or celebrating excessively after any play. Coaches should remind kids that this isn't acceptable and share feedback privately with individual players who behave this way. It's a team sport and actions, especially arrogant ones, that ignore that fact are usually frowned upon.

Final Thoughts on My Philosophy

Baseball is a game of failure. The absolute best professional hitters can fail to get a hit 7 out of 10 times and still be considered highly successful. Obviously, this can be extremely frustrating. To deal with this, good baseball players emphasize the process over the result. Hitting a hard line drive right at a fielder is a perfect example. The process was good—hitting the ball hard—but the result was "bad"—just another out in the scorebook. This can be handled one of two ways. You could bemoan your lack of luck or, with a process-oriented approach, consider the at-bat a success. You should focus on what you can control and ignore what you can't. Although it hurts your batting average in the short-term, if you're able to repeat this particular at-bat, this *process*, over the long run then it will result in many, many hits—a lot of good results.

This is just one way in which I believe that baseball provides kids an avenue to define and master qualities that will help them long after they've retired their cleats. Sure, baseball isn't a "lifelong sport" like golf or tennis but the lessons provided in a stable environment last just as long. I grew up in a tough area and baseball directed me in a positive direction. Looking back, I was particularly fortunate to get into catching. I turned out to have a talent for it, but it also taught me to communicate—to be a leader on the field and also how to interact with people on and off of the field. In a time today where kids can be consumed with iPads, smart phones, and electronic screens, actually conversing with someone face to face is a talent that is underdeveloped. Baseball has become more valuable than ever for honing interpersonal skills.

A quick story from my youth baseball days: when I was 12 years old something happened that changed my life and baseball career. I was a horrible teammate. I was kind of aware of it, but in retrospect, I really didn't know how bad it looked when I yelled at my teammates and acted up. I was intense, wanted to win and hated to lose and loved baseball but really didn't know how to conduct myself on the field yet. As a last ditch effort, my mother took pictures of me on the field with an old Polaroid camera and lays them out on a table when I came home. It was then that I finally realized that I needed to change. I never imagined how crazy I looked, with my face contorted and fraught in angles that it really shouldn't be.

Yes, baseball involves a lot of individual performance based on a team concept, but it is a team sport. And you have to learn how to process failure and defeat. How you treat your teammates and how you act between those lines matters because a lot of that can manifest itself in your everyday life. Conduct yourself in a way that you can be proud of, not one where you wouldn't recognize yourself.

This episode taught me a lot about leadership and staying positive for those around you. I learned to be a better teammate and leader. I was too focused on winning and myself and not the process and my team.

These habits—positive or negative—only become more prevalent when you get older. In college especially, kids are living on their own for the first time in their lives with more free time than they previously had. With no passion, this can become dangerous and habits can become destructive. I'm thankful that I had baseball or I doubt I would've had such a healthy and fulfilling college experience—all that excess energy would've been poured into something less worthwhile. At Binghamton, baseball took up a lot of my time, so I was forced to learn time management and discipline. I had to plan ahead or I knew I wouldn't be able to finish all my work or get to that early morning weight lifting on time. I have no doubt that this has aided me in my adult life in helping me to become a productive person, husband, father and small business owner.

Made in the USA
Monee, IL
19 June 2022

98272491R00085